Floyd's
India

SAFFRON

Floyd's
India

Keith Floyd

Location photographs by Kim Sayer

HarperCollinsPublishers

Thanks to:
Producer and Floyd's Manager: Stan Green
Director: Nick Patten
Production Manager: Wendy Rollason
Unit Co-ordinator: Adrian Worsley
Assistant Chef: Mariappan Sethurajapillai a.k.a. "Murry"
Camera: Mike Woods
Sound: Martin Alimundo
Researcher: Raj Ram
Stills Photographer: Kim Sayer
Official Observer: Tess Floyd

Special thanks to:
All the staff and management of:
Trident Hotel, Jaipur
Raj Vilas, Jaipur
Trident Hotel, Udaipur
Taj Fisherman's Cove Hotel, Nr Madras
Taj Malabar, Cochin
The Bombay Brasserie, London

Also, very special thanks to:
Tim Grandage and the street kids of 'Future Hope', Calcutta
(thanks for the Calcutta Cup Silver Rupee);
and Sanjay Galhotra, his family and staff who made us so welcome
at the M.K. Hotel, Amritsar.

And also thank you:
Emirate Airlines (specially the London ground staff!!xxx),
and Jet Airways, India,
and the poor sods who pulled the rickshaws all day,
and Ken and Ed and Beryl and Derek.

First published in 2001 by HarperCollins*Publishers*.

Text © Keith Floyd 2001
Location photographs of Keith Floyd and food photographs copyright
© HarperCollins*Publishers* 2001
Photographs on pages 48–49 copyright © Stan Green 2001
All other location photographs copyright © Kim Sayer 2001
Channel 5 logos are trademarks of Channel 5 Broadcasting Limited and
Channel 5 Broadcasting Limited 2000
Keith Floyd reserves the moral right to be identified as the author of the Work.

Keith Floyd is represented by Stan Green Management, Dartmouth, Devon;
telephone 01803 770046; fax 01803 770075. Visit www.keithfloyd.co.uk
The Channel 5 television series 'Floyd's India' is produced by Nick Patten Productions Ltd in
association with Stan Green Management.

Location photography: Kim Sayer
Studio food photography: Michelle Garrett
Home Economist: Carole Handslip
Commissioning Editor: Barbara Dixon
Designer: Mark Stevens
Editor: Felicity Jackson
Indexer: Susan Bosanko

A catalogue record for this book is available from the British Library.

ISBN 0 00 414088 5

Colour origination by Dot Gradations
Printed in Great Britain by Bath Press ltd

Contents

Introduction

Once upon a time a 14-year-old boy caught a perch in a lake near Bishop's Lydeard in Somerset. It was late summer, early autumn. There were blackberries in the hedgerows and beechnuts underfoot. In his tackle bag the young angler had a loaf of stale bread from the Golden Hill bakery in Wiveliscombe. This he soaked in water to make small pellets of bread paste for bait. He had cycled 12 miles from before dawn to be at the lake at sunrise. By noon his keep net contained six perch, one crutian carp and two small tench.

Contented, he opened the saddle bag on his bicycle to take out the sandwiches that his father had prepared. The thermos flask of coffee was there with a twist of blue sugar paper with sugar inside, but not the sandwiches. He had forgotten the picnic, but he did have a packet of 10 Nelson filter-tipped cigarettes and a box of Swan matches.

With his sheath knife, he scaled, de-finned and gutted a couple of perch. He cut some twigs from a tree and made things that later in life he discovered were kebab sticks. He picked blackberries and shelled beechnuts and stuffed them into the soaked stale bread, then he formed the bread into patties and toasted them over a fire of pine cones. He speared the fish on the twigs and sat cross-legged as he held them over the fire until they were cooked. With his hands, he ate the scorched fruit-and-nut-stuffed bread patties and succulent morsels of barbecued perch.

A hundred years later, by the most bizarre route, that boy became a restaurateur and what is obscenely called, not only obscenely but totally without justification, a television celebrity chef. Over 16 or 17 years he travelled the world, eating, cooking and learning, watching the legs being ripped off live frogs in a Singapore market, drinking the blood and the still-pulsating heart of a cobra in Vietnam, cooking salmon fishcakes wrapped in pig's caul in Northern Ireland, staring at the Southern Cross in the top end of Australia, eating ribs of beef and living in fear of being bitten by a king brown (one of the world's most poisonous snakes – Australia has eight out of ten of the most poisonous ones). He cooked pasta in Bologna, couscous in Morocco, moussaka in Greece, jambalaya in New Orleans, paella in Spain, bouillabaisse in France, dumplings in Prague, goulash in Budapest, puffins in the Arctic Circle, bear on the Russian border, carp in Czechoslavakia, hog's pudding and lava bread in Wales, salmon and haggis on the banks of the river Tay, Nile perch stuffed with raisins and nuts in Luxor, and freshwater crayfish cooked in beer in Sweden on a mad midsummer night. He prepared tom yang kum in Bangkok and beef rendang in Kotabura in Malaysia, stewed wildebeest in a *poiki* pot in Zambia, cooked cakes and schnitzels in Vienna, cooked pig's trotters (crubeans) and bacon and cabbage in Cork city, and the rest and more.

Weary of airports and hotel lobbies, taxis and studios, absurd locations and television directors, producers and book editors who know absolutely bog all about the subject (except that it is popular)[*not us, surely? Eds*], this boy – who is now a man but still remembers being 14 and remembers the words of Confucius, 'Give a man a fish and he will live for a day, teach a man to fish and he will live forever' – has had enough. He decides to move to the Mediterranean, where the olive, the lemon, the tomato, the aubergine and the wine are the jewels in the glittering culinary crown. Then, one fine day, he gets a fax, 'Go and do a series on India', it says. 'I don't know anything about India', he replies. 'Don't worry', they say. 'We will send you all the information. All you have to do is pop on to a plane and get cooking.' And so they did. The facts as presented to me by Nick Patten, my director, and my esteemed researcher, Raj Ram, I have incorporated into my letter from India that starts on page 12.

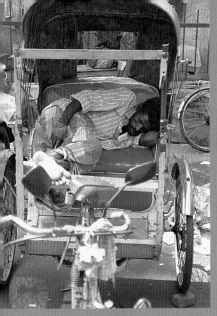

Letter from India

Letter from India

Kerala...sketches from coconut country

The big orange sun is rising slowly, illuminating the hazy morning as the plane begins a series of long, slow, gentle swoops downwards to Cochin airport in the southern Indian state of Kerala. Endless coconut plantations shimmer grey-silver, slate and green as the sun washes through whisps of cloud and beams on endless meandering waterways, alternately gold and silver, stretching far away. On the slopes there are coffee and tea plantations. Whitewashed colonial Portuguese or Dutch churches are scattered in clearings. Neat villas and verandahed farmhouses pop up in shafts of bright sunlight. Cows, bullocks and goats wander across extinct dried-up deltas that criss-cross the verdant landscape. The twisting waterways and lagoons give way to huge wide rivers and estuaries. Big rusting ships glide lazily along, while all manner of brightly coloured ferries, fishing boats and traditional craft, lanteen-rigged, double-ended, high prows and sterns sweeping up like a cobra poised to strike, sail serenely, outrageously overladen with mountains of hay or sculpted pyramids of coconuts, precariously but precisely stacked, edging steadily into harbour.

As the plane sweeps low over the water for its final approach, I can see loincloth-clad, sinewy men throwing big circular nets from the tiny narrow canoes under the long concrete bridge that the spans the mainland and Willingdon Island. The bridge is teeming with pedestrians, turmeric-coloured tuktuks and brightly painted, over-laden trucks piled high with hessian sacks of rice and pepper, coconuts or bananas.

Below *Images from Kerala.*

On top of their cargo, their backs to the oncoming traffic, sit the workers, huddled against the morning smog and dust, their mouths wrapped in bright bandannas.

Even at this early hour, the air is hot and slightly choking as we walk across the tarmac of the neat yellow airport. The runways are fringed with coconut palms and, although quite new, the airport buildings have the quaint, unhurried air of a genteel colonial outpost.

You present papers, tickets, passport and boarding cards several times to officials, soldiers and policemen. They are polite, insistent and bewildering. Behind the barrier in the baggage hall, hotel touts, porters, relatives, more soldiers, taxi drivers, nuns, hippies and beggars jostle. In the confusion I am met by two, but rival, chauffeurs, each sent by a different company to pick up Tess, my wife, and me and our 12 pieces of luggage. A polite man in a safari shirt and pressed chinos, carrying a clipboard and briefcase, settles the dispute, I think! But do I pay him too?

One driver will take Tess and me, and the other our luggage, but not before our trolleys have been hijacked by about six itinerant porters. Lesson one: carry bundles of small denomination notes or hold on to your luggage like hell and, more importantly, make sure the man who says he is here to escort you is genuine! They all want to take you somewhere, so don't arrive drunk or you may end up anywhere!

The aerial view I had enjoyed as we came into land appears. But soon we are bouncing along the centre left or right of the road, charging at oncoming window-less, garish buses like a wounded buffalo or swerving past on the inside of fume-belching trucks and weaving crazily between the streams of tuktuks, scooters and motorbikes, wildly and narrowly missing the oxen, buffaloes, cows and goats (goats, aka mutton, not lamb, on menus). Huge elephants, carrying their breakfast under their trunks – they eat about 300 kilograms of fodder per day – pad morosely towards their daily toil.

And all the while our driver, Johnny P.J. (as I came to know him in the course of our visit), has his hand firmly pressed on his five-tone horn.

I light up a fag, my first for hours, shut my eyes and hope for the best.

The tossing, turning, jolting, stomach-churning jeep slows down. After nearly an hour of relatively rapid progress, we are entering the morning rush in Cochin. The din, mayhem and confusion is infernal, yet strangely peaceful. There is a gentle feeling. Brightly clad women and neatly uniformed school kids walk steadily along the dusty streets. The stalls and shops are sleepily opening. Mud forecourts are being swept with short-handled stick brushes. The traffic is, in fact, not aggressive, it is just the noise from their horns, not the drivers themselves. It seems to be a case of let live, let die, but without malice of any kind. I ask Johnny P.J. if he knows somewhere good where we can stop for breakfast.

He shakes his head sideways, and a few moments later pulls up in front of a single-storey building on the corner of a very crowded junction.

'Why are we stopping?' I ask.

'You said breakfast.'

Above *Now that's a curried egg!!*

'But, you said No', I reply.

He shakes his head sideways again. I am beginning to understand. He opens the door and we duck into the low doorway of the Hotel Unikrishna.

Above faded red formica tables on spindly and teetery metal legs, three-winged fans spin lazily from stretched wires to stir the fetid air, while chattering loinclothed men squat, right-handedly eating their breakfast.

Waiters, barefoot or in sandals, carry steaming tin plates. In a corner behind a ramshackle *barthe* car (tea) boys juggle with long-spouted tin teapots, a huge urn of boiling milk and a cauldron of boiling water, pouring both milk and tea from a great height simultaneously into glasses and tin mugs with the panache of a New York city cocktail barman.

I have not been able to take curried eggs seriously as a dish because of the Goon Show catch phrase, 'No more curried eggs for me', but hard-boiled eggs masala – i.e. with a curry sauce – served with uppama (a cake of steamed semolina stuffed with curry leaves, mustard seeds and chillies) and coconut and coriander chutney (see page 174) is a terrific way to start the day. (In fact, I was so taken with spicy vegetarian Indian breakfasts that I did not eat a European-style breakfast for the entire two and a half months of my visit.)

There are other good dishes too, such as idli, a steamed rice sponge cake served with vegetable masala, chickpeas, lentils and potatoes in a rich onion and tomato-based gravy; appam, a rice flour pancake with spicy potatoes simmered in coconut milk and chillies; and idiappam, thin rice noodles garnished with grated fresh coconut, served with black bean masala. These and many, many other dishes are available for an average cost of a few pennies.

I drink fresh lime juice with soda and salt (if you like sweet drinks, thin honey can be substituted for the salt). The tea, made strong and with hot boiled milk, is too rich

for me. There are a dozen cooks in the lean-to shack that is the kitchen. It is fiercely hot and gloomy, with just a single light bulb hanging from the ceiling. Before a long low stone, through which blazes a fire fuelled by wood and coconut husks, the cooks squat, sweating over huge brass or aluminium pots, stirring the contents. They wear only a small piece of grubby sheet tied around their waist. In another corner a boy sits cross-legged, peeling and chopping a mountain of tiny, tangy red shallots. On makeshift griddles over wood fires, cooks are rolling out pancakes, cauldrons bubble and gurgle, and steam rises chokingly into the ceiling with the acrid taste of eye-watering wood smoke. The tin plates, once empty, are rinsed under a cold water tap mounted on the wall above an open drain. A veritable black culinary hole of Cochin and not a place for the weak-stomached or the faint-hearted.

After breakfast we visit the banana market and the produce market, which is dirty, fly-infested and stinking like the fetid, polluted river Styx, yet peopled by brightly dressed, cheerful shoppers who stare curiously, uncomprehendingly at me as I do the director's bidding. For example, buying a bunch of curry leaves four times from the same stall-holder, who has clearly not been on a television course – much to the frustration of Nick, the director – and, instead of obediently serving me in this absurd way (with no explanation as to why), keeps looking at the camera. A cardinal sin in a director's eyes!

Just as the stallholder has recovered from this bizarre intrusion into his daily business, Kim, our stills photographer, manifests himself from behind the bewildered crowd of onlookers and asks him to repeat the process. 'Please, just for me, if you don't mind. Thank you.' He clicks the shutter. The man relaxes.

'Just one more, please. No, please don't look at the camera. Just look at Mr. Floyd.'

I can sense him thinking, 'Who the........... is Mr. Floyd'.

'Thanks, lovely. I'm just going to change the lens.'

I can hear the man thinking 'Change the lens. For a bunch of curry leaves? Why the?!'

'Terrific, thank you. Now I'll just do a wide angle. No, don't look at the camera. Just explain to Mr. Floyd the joy of um...' (aside to me, 'What are those things?')

'Curry leaves.'

'Oh, yes, curry leaves.'

Click, click.

'Thank you.'

Throughout the hot, hazy afternoon we tramp round to the pepper exchange, take tuktuk rides and shoot emotive pictures of this bustling city. As the sun begins to sink, even Big Mike, the camerman, is wilting under the weight of his camera and the oppressive heat. Gratefully, we clamber into our vehicles and head, albeit slowly, through dense cacophonous traffic and the streaming pedestrians back to the tranquillity of our hotel, a bath, change of clothes, a stiff drink and dinner. We have been travelling and working since 3.00am. and by 9.00pm everyone in the crew has gone to bed. Tomorrow we start at 4.00am.

From the balcony of our room, I overlook the outlet of the Vembanad Lake, which flows into the Arabian Sea. Across the sound, the lighthouse flashes its pale light, occasionally illuminating a ghostly container ship slipping out on the night tide to the Middle East, Africa and beyond. The rooks that chattered so harshly in the red-flowered Mayflower trees are asleep and silent, and a security guard in a neatly pressed uniform is leaning against a tree having a smoke as he stares across the black water. I finish my drink and climb happily into a cool, firm bed.

Situated along India's southwest coast, Kerala is a lush, green tropical paradise. From the fabled Malabar Spice Coast, it stretches east to the mountain peaks of the Western Ghats. Kerala is 603 kilometres long but only 75 kilometres wide at its broadest point. The interior is riddled with inland waterways known as the backwaters, extending from the coast far inland and, as in Venice, these act as roads. Houses and schools are built on the banks and people travel by boat and bursting water buses. These areas are full of coconut palms and paddy fields – rice is Kerala's main grain and is eaten at every meal. Indeed, Kerala means 'Land of the Coconuts', and coconut is a common flavouring in the local food. Another widespread tree is the curry leaf tree, whose sweet and spicy leaves give the local dishes a distinctive aromatic flavour. The local flavourings of coconut and spices are combined with meat, fish and vegetables in dishes such as prawn ularthiyathu (prawns in coconut milk), beef ularthiyathu (a dry beef curry), or vegetable stew (called avial), traditionally garnished with quickly fried fresh curry leaves (see pages 114, 134 and 155).

The contrast between the little communities and villages clustered along the water's edge, or in cleared compounds under the coconut palms and cashew trees, and the city

Above *Hard work – but the coconut is essential in the Indian kitchen*

is strikingly vivid. The shallow waterways are covered in lilies and, as you glide past the little settlements with their neat gardens of vegetables and the black pigs, chickens, ducks and goats munching in the undergrowth, kids are playing cricket with home-made bats and bamboo sticks for stumps. Women, waist-deep in water, beat and rinse the washing. Men throw nets from narrow canoes. Huge, brilliant kingfishers swoop like Mirage jets just above the tranquil water and nilgiri birds – known as the laughing thrush – screech hysterically in the rich, tangled bamboo. School children, immaculate in blue shorts or skirts, white shirts and blue ties, clamber on to the little ferries that cross the river to take them home from school.

While rice and coconuts are the main crops, on the higher ground grow the more valuable coffee, tea, cocoa, rubber, pepper and cardamom. Kerala is the home of many spices and these have attracted merchants from all over the world. It is the natural habitat of black pepper and cardamom, and ginger and turmeric are also grown. India produces one third of the world's pepper and much of it comes from Kerala. Before the Portuguese introduced chillies into India in the 16th century, the Indians only had pepper to heat up their dishes. There is a interesting wholesale spice market in Cochin and the city also has the distinction of having the first church built by Europeans in India, St Francis Church, which was started in 1503. Tropical fruits are also abundant in Kerala, in particular pineapples and bananas, including the rare red-skinned variety that is supposed to be good for your health.

All the while, almost in a dream, I am sitting on the shaded deck of a highly polished and varnished rice barge, sipping a cool beer under a lazy fan, waiting for my meal of cabbage and mustard seeds cooked in coconut milk, beetroot with chillies, fresh coconut bread and chicken. This long, elegant craft once transported rice and fruits, nuts, bananas, hay or building materials the length and breadth of the area. In former times the hulls were fastened with coconut twine. Not a rivet or a

metal fastening was used and, on the open stretches, a single, huge, pregnant sail drew them gracefully along. Today, we drift gently along with a 25hp outboard motor fixed on the side, and where once the rice was stored, there are now quaint, charming, wooden bedrooms and a plant potted in a brass urn. This is paradise.

Or, rather, it would be if I did not have to do pieces to camera and pose, cheerfully, thoughtfully, happily or excitedly as I deliver what are supposed to be words rich in information, with wit and enthusiasm, and describe my food without speaking with my mouth full, or having a fag! OK, it's one hell of a job. But, as they say, someone has to do it.

Looming suddenly round the bend is a huge floating hay rick 6 or 7 metres high, amazingly piled on to a narrow-beamed, 12-metre rice boat. The hay overhangs the bulwarks either side. It has been loaded on to the boat with incredible precision and it passes us without the slightest wobble or even the remotest chance that it could topple over. One man is sitting smoking on the long-necked prow, another sits in the stern, his feet trailing in the water as he steers the tiny outboard engine that propels the vessel.

Apart from some birds laughing in the jungle and the lap of the water rushing under the hull, all is peaceful. Bugger the director. I think I'll have a fag and a slurp.

The deck hand places a bottle of Indian whisky, a bottle of mineral water and a bucket of ice on the mahogany table. The sun is going down fast over the Chinese fishing nets, their cadaverous cantilever limbs loom in a sinister way like huge praying mantises in the fast-falling dusk. The coastline is dotted with these vast fishing nets that were introduced to the area by merchants in the time of Kublai Khan. Consisting of five teak poles rising up to 30 metres in the air, they scoop up fish as they swim by at high tide. The nets are considered so valuable that brides' families even offer them as dowries in marriage.

Fish is the speciality here and makes up a large part of the Keralan diet. Munambam Harbour is the location of one of the many local fish auctions. Fishing boats that left in the middle of the night return in the late afternoon as the sun casts its golden evening hue over the Arabian Sea. Boats crowd the docks, five or six deep, and as soon as the day's catch hits the land the auction starts. The noise is terrific as buyers shout out prices and fishermen haggle over the value of the catch. The nearby prawn factory has no mechanisation at all. About 160 women squat on the ground, peeling prawns at lightening speed and sorting them into different sizes. They are paid by weight so they wield their sharp knives with superb precision and can peel up to 60 prawns a minute.

Soon the idyll is over and it is time to start the job for which I have travelled to India: to learn to cook Indian food. At 9.00am, two days later, I present myself to the executive chef of the luxury Taj Malabar hotel on Willingdon Island, M.A. Rasheed (where I am, of course, staying in unbridled luxury with Tess and the rest of the gang), put on my apron and begin to learn about masalas. Talk about walking over hot coals, more like walking over hot chillies!

Opposite *India's opening batsman, Lords 2012...*
Below left to right *Floating down the backwaters.*
Cooking on the beach. At the fish market.

Above *Give a man a fish and he will live for a day, teach a man to fish and he will live forever.*
Chinese proverb.
Chinese nets, Fort Cochin.

Goa

From Kerala we went north – to Goa. There we had a lot of fun on our brief visit. We stayed at the Taj Fort Aguada beach resort where we were given a fabulous bungalow which had been built, along with several others, specifically for visiting heads of state for a Commonwealth conference some years previously. I was quite tickled to be given the bungalow that Mrs Thatcher had stayed in. This was the second time our virtual paths had crossed. The last time was in the *bodegas* (cellars) of Gonzales Byas in Jerez, Spain where I was invited to sign a barrel in the hall of fame adjacent to a barrel signed by Mrs T. Please note this is not a sign of my political leanings in any sense of the word, but I think it is about time she came back as the President of Great Britain.

Goa is a tropical idyll with superb sandy beaches, which have made it a favourite winter sun destination. Colva Beach, 25 kilometres of pure white sands, is one of south Asia's most spectacular beaches. The beaches are, however, only part of the picture. Inland is a lush patchwork of paddy fields and coconut, cashew and areca plantations. Further east are the jungle-covered hills of the Western Ghats and the drier Deccan Plateau. The Dudhsagar waterfall on the Goa/Karnataka border is the second highest waterfall in India – 600 metres from top to bottom.

The tiny state of Goa feels quite different from the rest of India, due to the fact that for 451 years, while the rest of India was under Mogul and British rule, Goa was a Portuguese stronghold. The influence of the Portuguese occupation is plain to see through the charming brightly painted villas and farmhouses in the pretty towns and villages. It is this southern European influence that is said to account for the difference in the general attitude of its people and the food that they eat. Wherever you go, you can find traces of Portuguese domination. The food blends a Latin love of meat and

Below left to right *One of the many beautiful beaches in Goa. Panjim market. Marigolds in the Latin quarter.*

fish with India's predilection for spices. Goans add vinegar to many dishes, giving them a very distinctive flavour. Alcohol is also prevalent – more than 6,000 bars around the state are licensed to serve alcohol, including the local brew, Feni, a rocket fuel spirit distilled from coconut sap or cashew fruit.

Away from the coast are the ruins of the Portuguese capital Old Goa, a sprawl of Catholic cathedrals, convents and churches that draws Christian pilgrims from all over India. Soaring above the canopy of palm groves, the colossal, cream cathedral towers, belfries and domes welcome you to one of the finest groups of Renaissance architecture in the world. Further inland, the thickly wooded countryside around Ponda harbours numerous temples. Spices have always been one of the area's principal exports, even before the Portuguese arrived, and there are several large spice plantations around Ponda that can be visited.

Festivals celebrated in Goa include Id-ul-Fitr, in January/February, a Muslim feast to celebrate the end of Ramadan; the carnival in February/March, which is three days of Feni-induced mayhem, and Shigmo, held in February/March. This is Goa's version of the Hindi holy festival held over the full moon period to mark the onset of spring. It includes processions of floats, music and dancing, as well as the usual throwing of paint bombs.

In Goa it is quite funny to see that the pony-tailed, bandanna-wearing flower children of the sixties are now in *their* sixties and still having a ball, although the pony tails have turned grey or indeed white. It was here that we met a couple of excellent eccentrics, Derek and Beryl – he a retired stockbroker of the old school, and Beryl who was just lovely, kind, cheerful and totally passionate about India and the Indians. They spent six months of every year travelling throughout India. Because they were such long-standing guests of the hotel, they were accorded all kinds of privileges, one of which was an outrageously delicious mango chutney sent down from Mumbai specifically for their use. So, every night we would meet for evening tiffin – I don't care what you think tiffin is, as far as I am concerned it's a large Bombay Sapphire gin with tonic and fresh lime – and devour a pile of freshly made poppadoms covered in the best chutney I have ever tasted.

Oh, and by the way, talking about food, I recommend to you two great Goan dishes, the Goan lobster curry (see page 129) and the beef or chicken vindaloo (see page 135), a dish that bears no relationship to the ones that we all used to eat with a belly full of beer on Saturday nights many years ago.

Below *Betim fish market.*

Madras (now known as Chennai)

Back in the sixties in England, office dress code was relaxed on Saturdays and you could do your morning's work wearing a sports jacket or a blazer instead of the Monday-to-Friday suit. Chaps tended to wear their sports club ties and hastened quickly through their desks to be in the *White Elephant* by 12.30pm. They stood in their dozens, kit bags at their feet, foaming pints in hand. Boys drank I.P.A., the men drank Worthington E. Objective: to down as many pints as possible before piling into old bangers or shiny M.G.s and heading for one of the many Bristol Combination Rugby Football grounds where, in the amicable brutality of Club Rugby (Bristol Combination style) they would, in the hot and sweaty scrum, gag on the Worthington-flavoured farts, throw up at half-time, eat an orange and have a quick drag on a Senior or a Nelson.

After you had lost and taken the communal bath, diplomatic relations were restored between the two sides. Bruised and broken, as one they piled back into the motors and headed off to the memorial ground to watch the last 15 minutes of Bristol thrashing Cardiff or Llanelli, Harlequins or Coventry and, clutching more pints, you would wonder why Bill Redwood and John Blake had not been selected for the England side. As time went by, the bar got hotter, tales of Rugby daring got louder, pints were spilt, voices were raised, and birds were eyed but not pulled because they were for the great men of the Bristol 1st XV.

In those, some say, halcyon days, Bristol was in Gloucestershire and the pubs shut at 10.30pm, but, minutes away, across the Clifton suspension bridge was Somerset, where the splendid hostelries stayed open until 11.00pm and there was the possibility that the landlord might just serve one more after time as he rang the bell. Everybody,

Below left and right *Images from Madras.*
Middle *Cleaning silverware.*

by now, was in complete disarray. Everybody had probably drunk between 10 and 20 pints of beer since the first dignified pint in the *White Elephant*. Two or three would have fallen by the wayside, quite literally; some of the sensible ones would have returned to their wives, but the single guys were hungry. A leader always emerges at a time of crisis. It was the one who stood on the table, pint in hand, tie unknotted, shirt undone, who, bright eyed and sweating, called out 'Who's for the Curry House?' And so, once again, we piled back into the vehicles, more crowded than before because one or two had disappeared, and headed back over the Clifton suspension bridge, down to the city centre, past the bus station and along to Stokes Croft where a flickering yellow neon sign announced the existence of the Koh I Noor Indian Restaurant.

Inside the dining room, with its 14 tables standing on a slightly sticky, thick carpet, each table had a slightly soiled but very starched tablecloth. The walls were covered in tawdry flock and the exhausted waiters, in their stained dinner jackets which were almost a deep, dark green through years of wear, adjusted their clip-on bow ties and prepared for the onslaught. They had an air of resigned acquiescence. Each table was dressed simply with a salt and pepper pot and a stainless steel sugar bowl filled with white sugar lumps. The call was for – because that's all there really was – six chicken vindaloo, nine meat Madras, four plates of evil smelling, deep-fried, crispy Bombay duck and mango chutney and, of course, 15 pints of lager. The bewildered waiter wrote the order on a series of little duplicate pads and headed for the kitchen only to be called back by the blue-eyed fly-half with crinkly blond hair, who was training to be an accountant, and from his position of authority on the main table he would say, 'Make that 30 pints.'

Eventually, on white plates, the pungent curries and mountains of plain boiled rice arrived. There was, of course, not enough cheap stainless steel cutlery to go round. The Madras was hot, fiery and acrid, the vindaloo was diabolical. One by one, chaps would go to the bog but, one by one, they didn't return because the old hands knew that you could climb out of the window and then you wouldn't have to pay your share of the bill. So, every Saturday night was a mad Madras night.

Well, dear reader, that was in another time. It was before Indian restaurants became a culinary force to be reckoned with, before silver leaf garnished fragrant biryanis. It was before Britain had ever heard of a tandoor oven, but it was at a time not so long after India gained independence from Great Britain and the country was still awash with ex-colonials who wanted to continue eating their meat Madras or chicken Madras and their Bombay duck. In reality, the concept of a meat Madras is entirely a figment of the British imagination, but that is something I learnt much later in life.

In the meantime, and hoping to fulfil some kind of youthful gastronomic holy grail, I left the west coast full of anticipation for my visit to Madras. But, they've changed the name! Yes, okay, Madras was the first important British settlement in India and yes, quite correctly, the Indians have given it back its original name, Chennai, but how can you now go into your favourite curry shop after a hard game and say, '9 meat Chennais and 30 pints of lager, please'?

Above left to right *Taxis Madras-style. A little wood burner. In the paddy fields.*

Chennai is India's fourth largest city, the capital of Tamil Nadu. It is a young city by Indian standards. Its foundation in the 17th century by the East India Company also marked the foundation of the British empire. When the fortification – called Fort St George – was completed in 1640 the walls protected the East India Company's factory and other European trading settlements. Its function was to serve as a base for British agents to prevent local merchants controlling the price of goods. It later became the city of Madras. As it grew, the local Tamil people assigned the name Chennai to the city, whereas the British stuck to Madras. In recent years, however, it has been decided that the official name of the city should be Chennai.

The city is the home of curry powder, which was originally developed in Madras for the nostalgic British wishing to re-capture the flavours of India after they returned home from the Raj. Huge quantities of curry powder are still manufactured in machines that resemble concrete mixers, but it is all for export. No Indian cook would dream of using it.

British buildings dominate the area. The Ice House was built to store ice imported from Boston until it was used to cool the gin and tonics of the British residents. The Madras Club was built as a place where the British elite could drink the G & Ts. The chief reminder of colonial days, however, is the High Court, the largest court of law building in the world outside London. To the south, 20 hectares of narrow lanes form the city's largest market, Kothawal Chavadi, which includes a colourful fruit and flower section. On the outskirts of the city is Asia's biggest film studio complex, just beyond the jaws of a fake shark which guards MGR Film City. On this enormous site, funded by the state government, are 36 sets standing ready for use. Tourists are sometimes invited to be extras, especially in Raj-era films.

Now, in the intervening 40 years between eating my first meat Madras and my first visit to Chennai, I have learned a lot and I certainly was not expecting to find an

Above *Away from the crowded streets.*

authentic meat Madras in Madras, any more than I would expect to find a spaghetti Bolognese in Bologna or a chop suey in Beijing. These, and many other internationally known dishes are, again, concoctions created by bewildered ex-patriots. I did, however, expect to find exquisite food, but I was disappointed. As with all big cities the world over, it is hard – not to say nearly impossible – to find the gastronomic heart of that place. I stayed at the Connemara Hotel where they had a specialist restaurant devoted to the Chettinad cuisine, which is fiery, hot and spicy and should be delicious, but it was not.

Using all the resources available to me, I sought out the so-called good restaurants but, quite frankly, you will probably eat better in Southall or Birmingham, and that is not to mention how hard it is to put up with the inexorable poverty and squalor which gives birth to begging and harassment. So then you have to ask yourself, if you are finding this so offensive, why are you here in the first place. Well, the fact is the cooking in India can be one of the great experiences of life but it is best enjoyed at the home of Indians, no matter how rich or poor they might be. They treat their produce with such love and such care. They prepare their masalas with the same sort of love with which Van Gogh must have mixed his oils.

I spent some time at a magnificent palace where a family of four or six people were attended by over two hundred staff. The dichotomy lies in the fact that the poor can't afford to eat in restaurants, so there are just absolutely fundamentally basic squalid soup kitchens, while the rich are so well off they can afford to have cooks at home, so no matter what you read in the otherwise absolutely essential Lonely Planet *Guide to India*, take their restaurant entries with a pinch of chillies.

If you do eat in the streets of any of the big three cities, Chennai, Calcutta and Mumbai, and you choose a place which is very, very busy, you will usually eat well for a few pennies, cents or dimes.

However, if you are in Chennai, make a point of eating at Hotel Saravana Bhavan. This is the ultimate in Indian fast food restaurants. They have a menu of over three hundred different dishes, mostly vegetarian. They serve up to 4,000 meals a day (by the way, it is not a hotel, the word 'hotel' in many parts of India means restaurant or canteen). You get a tray on which are eight, nine or ten little dishes, savoury, sweet, hot, sour. It is called a thali (see page 76) and the first person who replicates this brilliant concept (in many ways not dissimilar to Spanish *tapas*) in London will make a fortune and change the gastronomic mindset of a nation already obsessed with Indian food. Anybody prepared to put several million quid into my idea can buy not only my expertise, my knowledge and my passion but they will also have the exclusive rights to the name of this amazing chain of eateries and, with due apologies to Paul Scott, it will be known as 'The Last Days of the Floyd'.

We ground out of Chennai through the appalling traffic to the village of Sriperumbudur where, from a distance, you can see water buffaloes bathing and high-rise ancient temples which, if you squint, remind you of Gotham City. We saw the ancient reservoirs, so-called tanks, where the lepers cleanse themselves and the locals do their washing, but it ain't like a visit to Salisbury Cathedral!

It was quite funny on the day that we all went there to film what is actually a very beautiful and fascinating place. On the way my beloved director, Nick, somehow got it into his head that the Indians grow a lot of rice and we should acknowledge that fact in our telvision programme. You have to remember, however, that there is nothing real in television land. Some 30 or 40 hapless Indian women were planting rice in a paddy field but, *quel horreur*, on the shady side of the field. This is, of course, totally unacceptable; for television purposes they must be in the sunshine to avoid shadows, so that the colours are bright and vibrant. To make matters worse, it was impossible to

Below *Sriperumbudur Temple and Tank.*

Above left to right *One of the many temples at Kanchipuram. Bogged down at Muttukadu.*

get a shot of these people from the road because the camera angle would not be correct. So, at the behest of Nick, our long-suffering researcher, Raj, was instructed to tell the *semailleurs* – which is French for seed sowers – to move over to the other side of the field and replant what they had already planted for the benefit of our camera. In the meantime, Stan, my manager, on this day dressed in combat kit, drawing on a cigar and for all the world looking like Stormin' Norman, hijacked and occupied the adjacent hospital. He stormed the operating theatre, where bewildered surgeons were bullied into allowing him – in mid-operation – to place the camera on the roof so that the world could see something that they have probably never seen before, since the dawn of television, a load of women planting rice.

Interlude at Kanchipuram

Some 40 or 50 minutes out of Madras there is a splendid Taj hotel called Fisherman's Cove at Covelong Beach, near Kanchipuram in Tamil Nadu. The beaches are unspoilt, there are spectacular views, regular rooms in the hotel complex and utterly enchanting guest bungalows on the beach. Here, with Tess, I spent six magnificent days as the guest of Sarabjeet Singh, the general manager. During that time I learnt how to make some exquisite dishes, including the subzi poriyal (crunch spicy beetroot with coconut) and kathirikai kara kulambu (a spicy aubergine dish) on pages 153 and 156, from the hotel's executive chef, Fabian. I seem to remember he had a couple of hits in the charts in the late fifties. (Joke! Rock-'n-rollers know what I mean.)

Kanchipuram is the Golden Town of 1,000 Temples, one of India's seven most sacred cities. Nowadays only 126 temples survive, but five of these are considered outstanding. They are closed between noon and 3.00pm and are best visited in the afternoon. On the same stretch of coastline as Covelong Beach is the famous Shore Temple at Mamallapuram, probably the best-known sight in southern India.

Above *A Bombay market.*

Bombay (now known as Mumbai)

So, on a high from the Fisherman's Cove, our culinary circus rolled on to Bombay (or Mumbai as it is now known), birthplace of Rudyard Kipling in 1865, and a city famous for its red double-decker buses. Home of the wealthy and glamorous, Mumbai is the commercial hub of India. Here there is a huge contrast between the rich and the poor. The city claims more millionaires than Manhattan, and there is indeed an almost ostentatious display of wealth, and yet two million people in the city do not have access to a toilet, six million go without access to drinking water and over half the city's population of 16 million people live in slums or on the street.

The huge natural harbour is the reason why commerce blossomed in Mumbai, helped by the opening of India's first railway line which started in Mumbai. Elephanta Island in the middle of the harbour has magnificent rock-cut cave temples, one of the city's main tourist attractions, and in February a festival of music and dance is held at these cave temples.

Mumbai is also the home of Bollywood, the Indian version of Hollywood, which produces more films than any other city in the world – 120 feature films per year. In

Below *The Gateway of India.*

Above left to right *Lunch box delivery.*

Mumbai you can still savour the glamour attached to the notion of going to the movies at one of the glorious art deco cinemas.

The city also has over 50 laughter clubs. Members gather in parks all over the city each morning and laugh themselves silly, in the belief that happiness and health are connected and drawing on ancient yogic texts that highlight the beneficial effects of laughter.

Mumbai has a unique lunch service. Hot lunches are delivered to workers in their offices direct from their homes by something akin to a postal service. Before noon, *dabbas*, ever-hot lunch boxes, containing a home-cooked meal are collected from residencies by *dabbawallas*. They are sent to the city by train and dropped at various stations for lunchtime delivery by other teams of *dabbawallas*. Ownership and location of each lunch box is identified by markings decipherable by the *dabbawallas* alone. After lunch the whole process is reversed.

Crawford Market and the bazaars of Kalbadevi and Bhuleshwar sell everything from mangoes to tobacco to Alsatian puppies; if you can eat it or stroke it, you can probably find it here.

We stayed at the Taj Mahal Hotel on the waterfront next to the Gateway of India, a huge triumphal arch built in 1924 to commemorate a visit by George V and Queen Mary. The last of the British troops leaving India by sea passed through this arch. Nowadays the massive stone arch is used mainly as an embarkation point for ferries taking tourist to the Elephanta caves or down the coast to Goa. According to the Lonely Planet *Guide to India* (quote) Places to stay – Top End, 'The Taj Mahal Hotel, next to the Gateway of India is one of the best hotels in the country ... the Taj is second home to Mumbai's elite and has every conceivable facility, including three quality restaurants, several bars, a coffee shop, swimming pool, gymnasium and nightclub.' While I am the greatest fan of the Lonely Planet guides, I can only disagree with their description of the Taj Mahal Hotel – I think it is the worst hotel I have ever stayed in.

Above *The original flying dhobi.*
Opposite *Bombay Duck on Gorai Beach; not duck at all, of course, but dried, salted fish.*
Its pungent flavour is definitely an acquired taste.

One of the few delights of staying in an Indian hotel is the excellent laundry service. My grease-splattered, turmeric-stained shirts would come whizzing back, splendidly clean and immaculately pressed, and very quickly and cheaply too. But, they are not washed in gleaming Launderettes – they are literally flogged clean in Bombay's municipal laundry, locally known as the Dhobi Ghat at Mahalaxmi. Here, in a labyrinth of open-air stone and concrete basins, thousands of men scrub, wash, rinse and dry tons of dirty clothes brought from all over the city all day. Then, after they have been through hand-operated spin dryers, the clothes are spread out on some rusty old roof to dry, after which they are immaculately pressed, with charcoal-fired smoothing irons. You get a great view of this phenomenal place from the railway bridge near Mahalaxmi Station which is five stops up from Churchgate Station.

Rajasthan...of polo, midnight feasts and other stories

The whole crew – Mike the cameraman, Martin the sound recordist, Nick the director, Wendy the production manager, Raj the researcher, Stan the producer, Adrian, Stan's assistant, nurse and transport manager, Murry, my Indian chef, my wife Tess and myself had found it really hard going in Mumbai but everyone was in immensely high spirits as we boarded the plane to Jaipur in Rajasthan, despite the fact that it was Indian Airlines. By the way, if you are travelling internally in India, whenever possible use Jet Airways – a superb privately owned airline and one that serves excellent food (in Club class anyway!).

Rajasthan in northwest India may be a desert state, but it is bursting with colour and exuberance. Jaisalmer is by far the oldest Rajput city. Its imposing fort, built in 1156, is like a city in itself, with houses, shops, hotels and the towering maharaja's palace. The fort resembles a giant golden sandcastle rising out of the desert, like something out of the *Tales of the Arabian Nights*. The beauty of the Jain temples here also leaves visitors breathless. One of the largest festivals in Jaisalmer is the desert festival in January and February when villagers and townspeople don traditional garb, the camels are elaborately decorated and there is traditional dancing and music and camel polo. The Mr Desert competition attracts a swag of mustachioed hopefuls. It is an ideal time to visit the local sand dunes. *Bati* is a popular Rajasthan bread, traditionally buried in the sand and left to bake in the scorching desert sun.

Jaipur, the capital of Rajasthan, is called the Pink City, although in fact it is terra-cotta-coloured. It was painted in the traditional Indian colour of welcome in honour

Below left to right *The elegant women of Udaipur in traditional colours. 'L' – isn't that so, Charles?;Hawa Mahal (The Palace of Winds).*

Above *Madame Masala, I presume? Jai Samender.*

of the visit of Prince Albert in 1883 and has remained that colour ever since. Founded by Maharaja Sawai Jai Singh II in the 1720s, it is a regal city with bustling bazaars, beautiful architecture and colourful citizens and, despite neglect, overpopulation and chaotic traffic – and traffic means rickshaws, trucks, motorcyles, bicycles, cars, lorries, elephants, buffaloes, camels, cows, dogs, mules, goats and, of course, thousands upon thousands of pedestrians – it is a delight to visit. Take the Hawa Mahal or Palace of Winds, for example. This is a folly in the grand manner. It is not a palace at all, but a five-storey wall of windows that was built as a grandstand for privileged ladies to observe the streetlife and processions below while the west wind blew gently through its 953 glassless windows to keep them cool. Today it is a museum.

Throughout history, feuding Maharajas, Arabs, Persians and Turks all tried and failed to conquer Jaipur. This is because the city is surrounded by strategically placed forts linked by a wall 16 kilometres in circumferance. Even the British did not conquer the place; they just came to a cosy financial deal with the ruling Maharajas. The place is littered with spectacular palaces and even I, as a confirmed non-tourist, thoroughly enjoyed visiting them. Part of the City Palace is still the residence of the former ruling family. It is also great fun to hire an elephant and plod up to the Amber Fort.

Another bonus in Jaipur was discovering – rather too late on our journey – the hotels operated by the Oberoi and Trident group. The Oberoi hotels are dead posh and the Trident hotels are dead good, and I became firm friends with both the manager of the Trident, Tufan Ghosht, and the head chef, Sandhu. It was Sandhu who taught me how to make the perfect biryani (see page 70), along with many other dishes. One of the highlights of our stay there was meeting another two remarkable eccentrics in their late 60s, Ken and Ed, who stay at the Trident for six months of every year. Every evening they dressed for dinner in a different, sumptuous Indian costume. How their wrists had the strength to support their outrageously jewelled rings, I really can't imagine. To occupy themselves in the daytime – that is to say when

Above *The Lake Palace, Udaipur.*

they weren't shopping for exotic jewellery, silver, *objets d'art*, clothes and bits and pieces for one of their many exotic houses around the world – Ken worked, without pay, in the hotel laundry while Ed, dressed in immaculately tailored chef's whites, with his elegant Salvador Dali moustache, wafted around the kitchen and dining room for all the world as if he was Escoffier himself. For his own amusement, much to the delight of the chef, the manager and the rest of the staff, he, in his unpaid capacity as a visiting regal gastronome, made muffins and exquisite cakes.

I spent a diverting evening playing elephant polo, which is apparently unique to Jaipur, because, you see, when the Maharajas of Jaipur weren't shooting tigers, playing roulette and backgammon or entertaining the Prince of Wales or Jackie Kennedy, they had the odd chukka on elephants. This dynamic and fast-moving game (sic) has been played, I am told, in Jaipur for 300 years. Needless to say, vast wagers were placed but it was only after the Maharaja of Jaipur lost a load to the Maharaja of Jodhpur that he added this very pertinent rule to the game: 'No elephant may lie down between the goal posts.'

The best bit of our sojourn was when Tess and I, Sandhu, Tufan, Ken, Ed and a few other friends broke into the Tiger Fort in the dead of night. It was a startlingly clear, starry sky and from high on the hill the twinkling lights of the whole city of Jaipur were spread beneath us. Ed brought the cakes, Sandhu brought the tandoori kebabs and nan bread, Tufan brought the beer and I brought the whisky. Four hours later we woke up the driver of our limousine, who was asleep on the roof, and made it back to the hotel for a substantial breakfast of sambar, a delicious spicy, hot, lentil-based curry, washed down with foaming glasses of iced, salted lassi.

We were very sad to leave Jaipur, but they telephoned ahead to our next Trident hotel in the lake-city of Udaipur. There, chef Pradeep and all the staff made us incredibly welcome, and the success of many of the dishes I cooked I owe to the teachings of chef Pradeep. We had a fine time. The state of Rajasthan gets my vote as the best region of India both for the hospitality of the people, the excellent food and the magical sense of history and Indianness.

Above left and right *The City Palace Udaipur. Sunset at the Lake Palace, Udaipur.*

Travelling south from Rajasthan you enter the state of Gujarat, India's most westerly region. Its coastal location on the edge of the Arabian Sea and the Gujaratis' flair for maritime and mercantile pursuits has meant that the state has always enjoyed good trading, enabling the wealthy rulers to build fabulous palaces and temples with their trading profits.

Water has always been precious in the desert and semi-desert areas of Gujarat. In medieval times, when the kings of the region discovered an underground spring they protected it by housing it in an elaborately carved structure known as a step well. Instead of rising upward, a step well – a kind of mini palace – spirals down, burrowing into the earth to the source of the precious liquid. One of the finest examples is Adalaj Vav, a 15th-century step well, 20 kilometres north of Ahmadabad, the one-time capital of the state.

In the far south of the state, about 40 kilometres north of Somnath, is the Sasan Gir National Park, a lion sanctuary that is one of the last places in the world where Asiatic lions can be seen in their natural habitat.

In Gujarat the main crops are grains and pulses. Instead of rice, you find breads and pastas and noodles made from chickpea flour.

Above *The Amber Fort, Jaipur.*

Calcutta and West Bengal

In the 18th and 19th centuries Calcutta was known as the city of palaces. People still live in the crumbling skeletons of these palaces which can be found all over the city. Calcutta is a living museum of 300 years of architecture. It is also the intellectual capital of India.

Mark Twain described Calcutta's weather as being hot and humid enough to make a door knob mushy. In fact, the air in West Bengal is so humid that every form of greenery, bananas, aubergines, marrows, flat beans and rice (which is the staple here) grow in abundance.

West Bengal sits just above the Bay of Bengal and its main river, the mighty Ganges, breaks into dozens of rivers and rivulets before it flows into the sea just to the east of Calcutta. These rivers provide the area with its other staple – freshwater fish. The Manik Tala fish market is situated in the north of Calcutta, the oldest part of town, and by 6.30am it is already in full swing. Many of the fish are sold alive, making them hard to weigh as they leap around the scales, but the Bengalis will not buy them any other way.

Calcutta was the formal capital of the British Empire of India until 1911 when the capital was moved to Delhi. The British brought with them many new foods, including potatoes, for which the Bengalis invented hundreds of new recipes. The main cuisines here are Bengali and Anglo-Indian. There are two sorts of Bengali foods in Calcutta – Golhi and Bengali. Golhi food is eaten chiefly in the north of the city. Golhis do not eat chillies and love sweets. Bengal food is eaten by Bengalis originating from east Bengal; the dishes are the same as Golhi food but with added chillies and with hardly any sugar in the desserts. Bengali food is based on fish and a variety of sweetmeats; strict vegetarian taboos are not generally followed.

Opposite *Why do I think of Spike Milligan?*
Below *The crew at the Victoria Monument, planning the next action.*

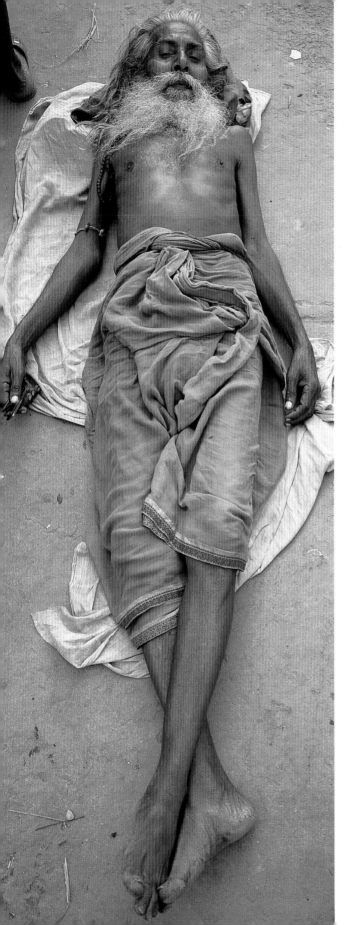

Calcutta is also famous for its hawker food. Hawkers, who are known as *punchkawallers*, are found all over the city and particularly near commercial centres to feed the lunchtime trade.

The waterfront of the Holy Ganga is the centre of the city's religious life. Every day, early in the morning and at sunset, people gather for ritual ablutions at the temples on the river's shores. In the south of the city is the Kali Temple at Kalighat, dedicated to the city's patron goddess, where goats are sacrificed on a daily basis.

One of the city's most original monuments is the Memorial to the Dead Telephone, built in 1984 by the Telephone Consumer Guidance Society of India. Every year a mourning ceremony is organised here to mark the collapse of the city's telephone network.

The sport of polo in its international form originated in Calcutta. The Calcutta Polo Club, formed in 1863, is now the oldest in existence and its red and white collars are used to decorate the goal poles of polo grounds all over the world. The season lasts from November to early March.

New Market, just north of Sudder Street, has the best florists and cake shops, and for caged birds and tropical fish go to Hati Bagen, further north, on a Sunday. At Sonapatti, goldsmiths sit cross-legged on the floor before huge iron chests. Here gold ornaments are bought and sold, exchanged and melted down, and precious gems and pearls are sold by weight.

Despite its elegant city centre, and although the Taj Bengal Hotel has splendid rooms and its lunchtime buffet is pretty good, the thing I found most fantastic in Calcutta was the book market. If you are in Calcutta, take a trip to Chuckervertty, Chatterjee and Co. Ltd. at 15 College Square, where you can buy everything from HG Wells' *War of the Worlds* to Malcolm Lowry's *Dark as the Grave Wherein my Friend is Laid.*

While in Calcutta, I had a spectacular day with a charitable organisation called Future Hope, who rescue abused street children from the gutters and from abuse, and help them to become confident, articulate and positive young people. They invited me to a Rugby match where they played their former enemies, the Calcutta police, and presented me with one of the original 19th-century silver rupees from which the famous Rugby Calcutta Cup was made.

Below *Ablutions on the banks of the Ganges.*

The Punjab

From Calcutta we flew to the Punjab, the rich, fertile plain in the north of India. The Punjab produces wheat for breads (bread rather than rice is the staple food), sugar cane and milk for dairy products. Fat (and I may say incredibly ugly) water buffalo are milked by hand and give a rich milk that is used to make tea, yoghurt, butter, cheese and ghee. About 85 per cent of the region is under cultivation and 70 per cent of the population work in agriculture.

The Punjab is probably best known in England, and in India, for its tandoori dishes (see page 100). The food is cooked in a tandoor, an oven shaped like a conical tube made of sun-baked clay, heated with wood or charcoal to produce a fierce heat that cooks food very quickly without drying out. The origins of the tandoor remain unclear, but they have been around in the Punjab for many centuries.

Tandoor ovens are made in Amritsar (just behind the bus station, an essential piece of information) from a mixture of clay and hay (and they cost very little). If you don't want to cook your own food, the (supposedly best) tandoori chicken in the Punjab can be found at Surjit's Chicken house, in Amritsar. Don't dress up for the occasion, in reality it is just a tiny stall.

Although Chandigarh is the state capital, Amritsar is its largest and most famous city – home to the famous Golden Temple, the holiest of Sikh shrines. It is constructed entirely of marble and gold and sits in the middle of a lake. The Punjab seems to be the larder of the continent. If nothing else, there is always free food in the Sikh temples. At the Golden Temple the mass feedings seem almost miraculous, the many doors to the feeding hall open in unison until 3,000 people are seated around the tables (in reality the floor!) leaving the rest to wait until the next seating. They only

Below *Getting about in the Punjab.*

Above *The restored Golden Temple – quite magnificent.*

have to wait half an hour, in that time the current seating is fed, the floor swept and the whole process starts all over again. That's India for you!

I hope my brief tour of India has helped to give you a glimpse of the sights and scents of this fascinating country and that your mouth is watering in anticipation of tasting the true flavours of Indian food. Now it is your turn to get cooking, using the authentic and traditional recipes I have collected from all corners of India.

The Recipes

The Indian subcontinent covers three million square kilometres, ranging from the soaring Himalyas to the plains, from tropical forests to deserts, with a long coastline of glorious beaches. The climates vary from the cool north and the temperate southern foothills of the Himalayas to the tropical climates of the western and southern regions.

India is home to about a billion people of various races and religions – Hindus, Muslims, Christians, Sikhs, Jains, Buddhists, Parsis and other minor sects – and the country's cuisines are as diverse as its culture, racial structure and varied geographical conditions. The Hindus do not eat beef – since cows are sacred to them – and many do not eat meat at all, while the Muslims eschew pork. A fair amount of lamb and goat is eaten. The cooler areas of the north are suitable for rearing sheep, and here lamb dishes such as biryani and rogan josh (see pages 70 and 145) are a speciality. In parts of the west many ethnic communities are strict vegetarians and this has resulted in wonderfully diverse vegetarian cuisines. Often vegetables are cooked with coconut in dishes such as okra sautéed with coconut (vendakai poriyal) and spicy vegetable curry (avial) (see pages 152 and 155). Vegetables vary with region and season, and the style of cooking is determined by the cereal or main dish with which they are served. Other important ingredients are milk and milk products, particularly ghee (clarified butter).

Common to all cuisines is the belief that food is a serious business – a gift of the gods to be treated with respect – and a characteristic of all Indian cooking is the inspired use of spices, not just for flavour, but also as appetite stimulators and digestives.

A word of caution

While I have done my level best to ensure that the recipes in this book work, I must tell you that as I cooked them – and indeed I have cooked every single recipe that appears in this book – I did not have the luxury of a fitted Smallbone kitchen complete with scales, timers and efficient gas or electric ovens. For the most part, I did not even have a kitchen and my cookers, such as they were, were improvisations worthy of Heath Robinson. One day I would be cooking with dried cow dung in a hole in the ground, another burning my wrists whilst attempting to slap Indian bread into a searingly hot tandoor oven. Most of the time I cooked over charcoal, and when I did have the luxury of gas burners they were either too feeble and would blow out with the slightest puff of wind or they were so fierce that they almost melted the saucepans. What I am trying to say is please approach these recipes with a good common sense attitude. All the measurements, timings, temperatures, quantities, etc., etc., are very approximate. If, say, a recipe calls for a tub of yoghurt, buy two just in case you need a little more. Do not slavishly follow the quantities of the spices for the masalas; you might like it hotter, in which case add more hot spices; you might like it a little milder, in which case leave out some of the chillies, and so on and so forth. It is just not possible to say that a lamb curry takes exactly 45 minutes. If you happen to be using very tender, young lamb it may only take 15, if you are using some tough old mutton or goat it may be an hour and a half. The thing to do is periodically taste and see how it is getting on. Anyway, I wish you very happy cooking and a contented tummy.

Masala

Madame Masala

her mysteries and magic

There are probably as many versions of masala in Indian cooking as there are sexual positions in the Khama Sutra, if not more... and, like lovemaking, real delight cannot be achieved without tender and exotic foreplay, so it is important to understand the subtlety required to prepare a masala before gorging on the delights of the tangy, spicy, pungent or creamy, fragrant or soft gastronomic sex that is Indian food. And, the base of it all is the masala.

Masala is a mixture of herbs and spices, whole or ground, that give Indian dishes their distinctive flavours when mixed and puréed with water, oil or vinegar, lime or lemon juice. The main spices and herbs in masalas include fresh green chillies, fresh ginger, garlic, red onions or – better still – small red shallots, fresh coriander leaves, fresh mint leaves, curry leaves, bay leaves, salt, hot dried Bird's Eye chillies, dried black mustard seeds, coriander seeds, black peppercorns, cardamom pods, cloves, cinnamon sticks, cumin seeds, fenugreek, fennel seeds, star anise, tamarind and turmeric.

Of course, you can buy all or most of the flavourings already ground to a powder, but, for the best results and for greater satisfaction, it is better to grind your own. A small coffee grinder for the dried spices and a small food processor for the fresh herbs is all you need. You will get even more flavour from the spices if you first lightly roast the seeds in a dry frying pan until they crackle, then grind them to a powder.

*Below left to right S*pice tray, from the top clockwise: hot chilli powder, cumin seeds, turmeric, cardamom pods, coriander seeds, cloves, mace. Savoi Verem Spice Plantation, Goa – cinnamon bark. Spice company.

Some recipes in this book use **dried powdered masalas**. In general, these should be gently stir-fried in oil for a few moments to eliminate the powdery taste before adding the recommended cooking liquid. Both wet and puréed masalas usually benefit from being stir-fried in a little oil first. Vegetable oil, coconut oil, mustard seed oil and ghee (clarified butter) are all used for frying. If you use mustard seed oil, do so sparingly as it has a strong, pungent flavour and a slightly acrid aroma.

Chillies were introduced to India by the Portuguese. The hottest ones are the small red Bird's Eye variety, and, as with green chillies, the more seeds you leave in, the hotter the flavour. Dried chillies too, like other spices, are more flavoursome if lightly roasted before using (either chopped, whole or ground).

Onions, ginger and garlic can either be chopped or puréed to a paste in a food processor. To make a **ginger and garlic purée**, combine, in most cases, equal quantities of peeled ginger and garlic and purée. To make a **brown onion paste**, finely slice or

Below *Coconut being cut out of its fibrous husk.*

Above *Karmali, Goa – pounding the spices for masala.*

dice some red onions, and sauté them in butter, ghee or oil until they are golden brown, then purée them in a food processor.

A **purée of tamarind** is often used for sour curries. This is very simple to prepare. Pop some tamarind pulp into a pan, cover with water and bring to the boil. Turn off the heat and leave to cool, then squeeze the flesh away from the seeds. Chuck the seeds away and process the liquid and flesh until smooth.

Many masalas, and indeed many dishes, use **coconut flesh**, either finely grated or thinly slivered. Dried coconut is generally a poor

Above *Spice trader in Jal Mahal market, Jaipur.*

substitute for fresh. In the south of India, in particular, **coconut milk** is used extensively to make the curry gravy (the term 'sauce' is not normally used) and is often made with freshly grated coconut flesh puréed with water and the liquid from the coconut. However, it is more practical to buy canned, unsweetened coconut milk from an Asian specialist. If the recipe calls for meat or chicken to be marinated or simmered in coconut milk, dilute the coconut milk with water and cook gently until the liquor has all but evaporated and then add the thicker milk to finish off the dish. If you start with the thick version, it will probably separate and curdle.

If you are able to obtain **fresh curry leaves**, you will find they add an exquisite taste to your dishes. Some recipes call for curry leaves to be crackled at the first stage of preparation. To use them to garnish dishes, quickly stir-fry the leaves in a little oil, so they are a dark, glistening, green colour and very slightly crispy. Small pieces of kaffir lime leaves are a reasonable substitute. If only dried curry leaves are available, use them in the gravy, but not as a garnish. Chopped fresh coriander leaves can be used as a good general garnish.

Some curries in this book are wet and some are dry. Quite simply, a dry curry is cooked with very little liquid, resulting in the morsels of meat, fish or whatever being coated with the masala gravy rather than swimming in it. (Most Indians eat with their fingers and mop gravies up with breads or balls of rice.)

Where masalas are used in the recipes, I have listed the ingredients and method as required for each individual dish. However, here are four all-purpose masalas for the cunning curry cook who is pressed for time. They are useful because they can be prepared in advance and stored in the fridge or in the freezer and, as long as you have some coconut milk and chutney in the cupboard, all you have to do on your way home is pop into your favourite store and buy yoghurt, fresh coriander and some meat or fish and you can amaze and impress your friends with a dish that tastes convincingly authentic. Thus, I offer you:

Above *I hate photos like this! It was taken at the Jal Mahal Temple, in Jaipur.*

Floyd's green masala

1 tablespoon coriander seeds

1 tablespoon ground turmeric

½ tablespoon cumin seeds

½ tablespoon cloves

1 cinnamon stick

a handful of fresh green chillies, coarsely chopped

a few cloves of garlic, peeled

a finger-sized piece of root ginger, peeled

1 cup of chopped red shallots

1 small sprig of fresh mint

1 bunch of fresh coriander leaves

a little sugar

salt

white wine vinegar, rice vinegar or water

1 Dry roast all the dried spices in a frying pan over a low heat, stirring, until they crackle.

2 Put all the ingredients into a food processor with a little vinegar or water and grind to a smooth paste. Pop the mixture into an airtight bottle or plastic food box and store in either the fridge or freezer.

3 To use the masala, heat some oil in a *karai* (Indian for wok) or any suitable pan, stir in the masala and cook for a few minutes. To make a gravy, add either water or coconut milk (dilute the coconut milk to start with, one part coconut to two parts water, to prevent it curdling when brought to the boil). Add meat, fish or vegetables of your choice and simmer gently until cooked. For the best results, use meat or chicken on the bone chopped into bite-sized pieces. The meat is put into the gravy raw, not sealed in oil as is normal in French cooking.

Floyd's red masala

a handful of dried red chillies

1 tablespoon cumin seeds

1 tablespoon black peppercorns

1 tablespoon ground turmeric

1 tablespoon cloves

1 cinnamon stick

1 large piece of root ginger, peeled and
  chopped

10–15 cloves of garlic, peeled

a little sugar

salt

red wine vinegar or water

Make, store and use in exactly the same way
as Floyd's green masala (see opposite).

Chaat masala

This is a salty and sour spice mix
and is sprinkled over cooked or raw
dishes to add flavour. Use it like salt
and pepper.

1 tablespoon cumin seeds

1 tablespoon black peppercorns

5 cloves

½ tablespoon dried mint leaves

¼ teaspoon asafoetida powder

2½ tablespoons dried mango powder

1 teaspoon powdered ginger

1 teaspoon chilli powder

¼ teaspoon tartaric acid

1 tablespoon rock salt

2 teaspoons sea salt

Lightly toast all the ingredients except the salts
in a dry pan. Add the salts and grind all the
spices while they are still warm in a coffee
grinder or food processor. Store in an airtight
container.

Garam masala

3 tablespoons cumin seeds

2 tablespoons coriander seeds

four 5 cm/2 inch cinnamon sticks

10 green cardamom pods, slightly
  crushed

10 cloves

½ a nutmeg, grated

3 blades of mace

1 tablespoon black peppercorns

3 star anise

4 or 5 bay leaves

1 Dry roast the spices and bay leaves in a frying pan over
a low heat, stirring until you can smell the spices.
Remove from the pan and allow to cool slightly.

2 Transfer the mixture to a coffee grinder or food
processor and grind to very fine powder.

3 The masala can be kept in an airtight container or it
can be frozen in a bag.

Rice

The Vexed Subject of Rice

Any kid from Bangkok to Calcutta, from Saigon to Bombay can cook rice. But, we Brits have trouble even cooking the boil-in-the-bag variety. Indeed, I know talented chefs who tremble at the thought of having to cook perfect rice and, when it comes to cooking dishes such as paella and biryani, I have seen pompous foodies cringe and tremble at the task. In the following dishes, the rice is thoroughly washed under running water until all the starch has gone before it is cooked.

Above and opposite *Rice shop, Palavakkam.*
Below *Madras paddy fields.*

Fragrant lemon rice

It is worth going to a specialist (Asian) store and buying the most expensive long grain rice you can find for this dish.

serves 4

1½ cups long grain rice, washed under
    running water for at least 15 minutes
    and strained

salt

ghee

vegetable oil

1 teaspoon black mustard seeds

small handful of fresh curry leaves

½ teaspoon finely chopped root ginger

1 green chilli, finely chopped

3 or 4 dried red chillies, coarsely
    chopped

1 heaped tablespoon unsalted cashew
    nuts

½ teaspoon ground turmeric

juice of 2 lemons

chopped fresh coriander leaves,
    to garnish

1 Boil the rice in plenty of salted water, giving it one quick stir once it has come to the boil. Continue cooking until the grains are just tender. Drain thoroughly, transfer to a bowl and stir in a heaped tablespoon of ghee. Set aside.

2 In a large shallow frying pan or wok, heat some oil. Add the mustard seeds and cook until they crackle. Add the curry leaves, ginger, chillies and cashew nuts and quickly stir-fry. Sprinkle in the turmeric. Stir in the lemon juice, a pinch of salt and about ¼ cup of water. Simmer the mixture for 2 or 3 minutes until you have a turmeric-coloured gravy.

3 Stir in the rice and continue cooking until the liquid has been absorbed and the rice is completely tender. Garnish with chopped coriander leaves and serve.

Right *Fragrant lemon rice*

Coconut rice

With brilliant rice dishes like this one who needs meat or fish? A plate or a bowlful of this eaten with some fresh Indian bread, some pickles or chutneys and Kachumber (see page 176) makes a delightful lunch or supper.

serves 4

250 g/9 oz basmati rice, washed under
    running water for at least 15 minutes
    and strained
salt
150 g/5 oz freshly grated coconut
vegetable oil
1 teaspoon black mustard seeds
4 or 5 dried red chillies, coarsely
    chopped
2 or 3 green chillies, coarsely chopped
2 cloves of garlic, peeled and finely
    chopped
2.5 cm/1 inch piece of root ginger,
    peeled and finely chopped
4 or 5 cardamom pods, crushed
a small handful of fresh curry leaves
1 teaspoon ground turmeric
salt
1 heaped tablespoon ghee

for the garnish

a handful of chopped fresh coriander
    leaves
slivers of fresh coconut (optional)

1 Put the rice into plenty of salted water, bring to the boil and cook for just 5 minutes, drain and then spread out on a shallow baking tray so that it can cool quickly.

2 Toast the grated coconut in a dry pan over a low heat until golden brown.

3 In a large shallow frying pan or wok, heat some oil. Add the mustard seeds and cook until they crackle. Add the chillies, garlic, ginger and the cardamom pods and stir-fry quickly.

4 Add the curry leaves and turmeric and stir-fry for a few seconds. Stir in the coconut and rice and mix thoroughly. Season to taste with salt. Cook for 2 or 3 minutes.

5 Remove the pan from the stove, cover and leave for 1 hour, then stir in the ghee. Reheat the rice either in a microwave or sauté gently on the stove. Serve garnished with chopped coriander leaves and a few slivers of fresh coconut, if wished.

Right *Traditional dancers, Jal Mahal, Jaipur.*

Jodhpuri pulau

This rice dish is traditionally part of a thali selection (see page 76). Jodhpur, by the way, is the name of an Indian city not polo-playing trousers!

serves 6–8

50 g/2 oz split yellow or red lentils, washed

600 g/1 lb 6 oz basmati rice, washed
   under running water for at least
   15 minutes and strained

1 onion

vegetable oil

100 g/4 oz ghee

1 teaspoon cumin seeds

3 cloves

2 pieces of cinnamon stick

4 or 5 green cardamom pods

2 black cardamom pods

2 bay leaves

salt

Opposite *Jodhpuri pulau.*

1 Soak the washed lentils in fresh water for 3 hours and the washed rice for 1 hour.

2 Cut the onion in half and slice it very finely into half moon shapes. Heat a little oil and fry the slices until they are very crispy, then drain and put to one side.

3 Strain the soaked lentils and the rice. Heat a little oil and the ghee in a pan or *karai*, add all the whole spices and the bay leaves and stir while they crackle.

4 Stir in the lentils, then add the rice and stir gently so that all the grains are coated with the oil. Add just enough water to cover the rice and season with salt. Bring to the boil, then lower the heat and cook gently, stirring from time to time until the liquid is absorbed and the rice is cooked.

5 Serve garnished with the crispy fried onions.

Cumin-flavoured rice Jeera pulau

Cumin is an indispensable spice in Indian cooking and it gives an exquisite perfume to rice. Don't hoard spices – they do go stale; buy them in small quantities to suit your needs.

serves 6

500 g/ 1 lb 2 oz basmati rice, washed
   under running water for at least
   15 minutes and strained

50 ml/ 2 fl oz vegetable oil

20 g/ ¾ oz cumin seeds

1 teaspoon black peppercorns

1 bay leaf

5 broken pieces of cinnamon stick

4 green cardamom pods

1 heaped tablespoon of ghee or butter

salt

chopped fresh coriander leaves, to garnish

1 Soak the washed rice in fresh water for 30 minutes, then drain thoroughly.

2 Heat the oil in a shallow frying pan or wok, add the cumin seeds, peppercorns and bay leaf and cook until they crackle.

3 Tip in the rice, cinnamon and cardamom and stir-fry in the oil for 10 minutes, stirring continuously. Add 1 litre/ 1¾ pints boiling water, season with salt, cover and cook for 8 minutes. Stir the rice once and add the ghee or butter. Replace the lid and cook for a further 7 minutes or until the water has evaporated and the rice is tender.

4 Serve sprinkled with chopped coriander leaves.

Floyd's imperial biryani

This is a sumptuous dish of tender, spicy mutton cooked gently in fragrant rice. A celebration dish, it should be served for a very special occasion. It is best to have small pieces of good quality mutton and, if possible, on the bone. Lamb or goat can be used instead of mutton, if preferred.

serves 10

1 kg/2¼ lb basmati rice, washed under
    running water for at least 15 minutes
    and strained
350 g/12 oz ghee
salt
150 g/5 oz coarsely chopped red onions
100 g/4 oz flaked almonds
2 kg/4½ lb mutton morsels (or lamb or
    goat)
250 g/9 oz natural yoghurt
100 g/4 oz cream
100 g/4 oz cashew nuts
100 g/4 oz raisins
6 tablespoons chopped fresh mint leaves
8 tablespoons chopped fresh coriander
    leaves
2 tablespoons lemon juice
a pinch of saffron threads soaked in
    2 tablespoons water
a few drops of rosewater
plain flour
vegetable oil
150 g/5 oz finely sliced red onions
small packet of silver leaf, to garnish

for the masala

10 cardamom pods
10 cloves
4 blades of mace
10 g/⅓ oz ground cinnamon

for the purée

40 g/1½ oz root ginger, peeled
40 g/1½ oz cloves of garlic, peeled
2 teaspoons chilli powder

1 Soak the washed rice in fresh water for 1 hour. Meanwhile, dry roast all the spices for the masala in a frying pan over a low heat, then grind them to a powder in a food processor or blender. Mix together all the ingredients for the purée.

2 Drain the soaked rice thoroughly. Heat some of the ghee in a large wok or shallow frying pan and sauté the rice for 2 or 3 minutes until each grain is coated with ghee. Add enough water to just cover the rice (I emphasise you must only just cover the rice with the water). Season to taste with a little salt and then cook the rice gently until the water has evaporated. At this point the rice will still be slightly undercooked. This is correct. Remove from the heat and keep to one side while you prepare the mutton.

3 In a large heavy-based flameproof casserole with a lid, heat some ghee and fry the chopped onions. Stir in the masala powder and cook for 2 or 3 minutes, mixing well. Stir in the purée and cook for 2 or 3 minutes.

4 Stir in half the almonds, then add the mutton and season with salt. Stir in the yoghurt and a little water if the mixture seems dry. Cook gently until the mutton is tender and slightly dry. Stir in the cream and continue cooking gently.

5 Sprinkle half the cashew nuts, half the raisins and half the mint and coriander leaves over the mutton. Tip the rice on top, add the remaining raisins, mint and coriander leaves and mix them into the rice, and then level the top of the rice.

6 Sprinkle the lemon juice, saffron water and rosewater over the rice, then drizzle a little melted ghee over the top.

(continued on page 72)

Above *It took the director more time to get the elephants in the background than was given to me to prepare my dish, but that's television for you.*

Right *Some of the flavoursome ingredients that go into this magnificent biryani.*

Opposite *Jal Mahal, Jaipur.*

7 Make a stiff paste with plain flour, a little oil and water and knead it until it is like putty. Put a ring of paste around the edge of the casserole lid, making sure that there are no gaps. This will seal the casserole so that no vapour, steam or, more importantly, wonderful aromas can escape. Place the lid with its seal on the casserole and cook gently for 15–20 minutes.

8 Meanwhile, fry the sliced red onions in a little oil until they are crisp and golden. Put to one side. Fry the remaining cashew nuts and almonds in a little ghee until they are lightly toasted.

9 Just before serving the biryani, lay some pieces of silver leaf over the top and sprinkle on the toasted nuts and the crispy onions.

Thali

Thali

A thali is a tray, which can be pressed stainless steel or elaborately decorated gold or silver, upon which are placed a number of small metal dishes about 6–7 cm/2½–3 inches in diameter, again made of either stainless steel, gold or silver. The idea of thali is that the individual can sample several different dishes all at the same time. It is what the French would call a *menu de dégustation* and the Spanish call *tapas*, where the chef offers you small portions of all his favourite dishes. It enables you, should you wish and depending on what you put into your thalis, to have a multi-course meal, perhaps including a little soup to start, then going through a variety of vegetable or meat dishes and finishing with something like a mango kulfi (Indian ice cream). This is a fun way to experience Indian food and the first person who opens a stylish thali restaurant in London will make an absolute killing. As I recall my journey around India, I think that the only redeeming feature of Madras (or Chennai as it now is) was the fantastic thali fast food restaurant called Hotel Saravana Bhavan in a street called Dr Radha Krishnan Salai.

Any of the dishes in this book, with the exception of roasts, grills or tandooris, can be prepared and served as a thali. The following vegetable recipes I cooked for the manager of the Trident Hotel in Jaipur, my friend Tufan Gosht. Serve them with Jodhpuri pulau (see page 69), and Indian spinach bread (palak roti) (see page 83). Assemble your thali dishes so that each person will have on the thali tray four different vegetable dishes, one rice dish, one dish of raita (see page 173), and one dish of a pickle of your choice (see pages 172–179). If you wish to eat in the Indian manner, you can use the roti to scoop up the contents of your little thali dishes.

Simmered lentils Chana dal

You can use black, yellow, green, whatever lentils you like, but the important thing is you must first wash them well and leave them to soak in fresh water for an hour.

serves 4

200 g/7 oz dry lentils

1 teaspoon ground turmeric

salt

vegetable oil

1 heaped teaspoon cumin seeds

2 red onions, finely chopped

1 tablespoon mixed ginger and garlic
purée (see page 56)

1 tablespoon red chilli powder

3 tomatoes, finely chopped

for the garnish

chopped fresh coriander leaves

4 fresh green chillies

1 Cook the lentils with the turmeric and some salt in just enough water to cover until they are tender but not completely cooked and the water has evaporated.

2 Heat the oil in a *karai* or a saucepan, add the cumin seeds and fry until they crackle. Add the onions and sauté until golden brown.

3 Stir in the ginger and garlic purée and the chilli powder. Stir-fry for 2 or 3 minutes, then add the tomatoes and cook for 15–20 minutes or until you have a coarse purée.

4 Add the parcooked lentils and simmer gently until they are really tender. Serve garnished with chopped coriander leaves and a fresh green chilli per person.

Cottage cheese in spinach purée Sag paneer

Indian cottage cheese (paneer) is quite firm and can easily be cut into cubes. It is quite simple to make your own paneer, see page 183.

serves 4

400 g/14 oz paneer, cut into small cubes
vegetable oil
800 g/1¾ lb spinach, well washed
   and drained
knob of butter or ghee
100 g/4 oz ghee
1 teaspoon cumin seeds
2 or 3 cloves of garlic, peeled and finely
   chopped
2 teaspoons ground coriander
1 teaspoon red chilli powder
salt
100 ml/4 fl oz cream

1 Fry the cubes of cheese in a little oil until they are golden on all sides, then put to one side. Stir-fry the spinach with a knob of butter or ghee (no water is required), then purée it in a blender.

2 Heat the ghee, add the cumin seeds and as they crackle stir in the chopped garlic and sauté until it is golden brown.

3 Add the coriander, chilli powder and spinach purée. Season to taste with salt and cook for 3 or 4 minutes, stirring all the time.

4 Add the cubes of paneer and simmer gently to heat through. Stir in the cream and serve piping hot.

Baby onions stewed in yoghurt masala
Kande ki sabzi

Yet another dish that my culinary guru Sandhu showed me how to make while I was staying in Jaipur.

serves 4

100 ml/4 fl oz oil

1 teaspoon cumin seeds

1 heaped tablespoon mixed ginger and
   garlic purée (see page 56)

500 g/1 lb 2 oz baby onions of a uniform
   size, or medium red onions cut into
   quarters

for the masala

1 teaspoon red chilli powder

2 teaspoons ground coriander

2 teaspoons ground turmeric

about 50 g/ 2 oz natural yoghurt

salt to taste

1 Mix together all the masala ingredients with ¼ cup of water.

2 Heat the oil in a wok, add the cumin seeds and fry until they crackle. Stir in the ginger and garlic purée and cook for a moment or two.

3 Stir in the masala and then the onions, stirring thoroughly to ensure they are well coated with masala. Add about 1¼ cups of water and simmer gently over a low heat until the onions are tender but not losing their shape.

Opposite Thali tray – from top clockwise: Cottage cheese in spinach purée (page 79); Indian spinach bread (page 83); Mango and chilli chutney (page 178); Raita (page 173); Baby onions stewed in yoghurt masala; Simmered lentils (page 78); Potatoes with cumin seeds (page 82); Jodphuri pulau (page 69).

Potatoes with cumin seeds Jeera aloo

Indian cooks do not season their food or flavour their food, they temper their food – so this dish is really potatoes tempered with cumin seeds.

serves 4

vegetable oil

1 heaped teaspoon cumin seeds

20 g/¾ oz mixed ginger and garlic purée
   (see page 58)

1 teaspoon red chilli powder

salt

500 g/1 lb 2 oz parboiled potatoes, peeled
   and cut into 2.5 cm/1 inch cubes

for the garnish

1 teaspoon ground coriander

1 teaspoon garam masala (see page 63)

chopped fresh coriander leaves

1 Heat some oil in a *karai* or frying pan, add the cumin seeds and fry until they crackle. Stir in the ginger and garlic purée and sauté until it goes slightly brown.

2 Stir in the chilli powder and add enough water to make a gravy with a smooth, sauce-like consistency. Season to taste with salt.

3 Add the potatoes, mix them well into the gravy and simmer gently until they are tender.

4 Garnish with the ground coriander, garam masala and the chopped coriander leaves and serve.

Indian spinach bread Palak roti

Oh, Indian bread is so delicious but it's unrealistic really and truly for us poor Westerners to achieve the authentic taste because we don't have the tandoor oven. Should you wish to purchase one, I tell you how on page 101.

makes 6

oil
1 teaspoon cumin seeds
50–60 g/2–2½ oz chopped cooked
    spinach (weight after all the water has
    been squeezed out)
250 g/9 oz wheat flour
salt
melted butter or ghee for painting the roti

1 Heat some oil in a *karai* or frying pan, add the cumin seeds and fry until they crackle.

2 Mix the cumin seeds, spinach, flour and salt to taste and add enough water to make a tight dough.

3 Divide the dough into six portions and roll each one into a small ball, then shape them into discs with a diameter of 15–20 cm/6–8 inches.

4 Heat a griddle, plancha or a dry frying pan and toast the discs evenly on both sides.

5 Remove the roti from the pan and paint one side of each one with melted butter or ghee.

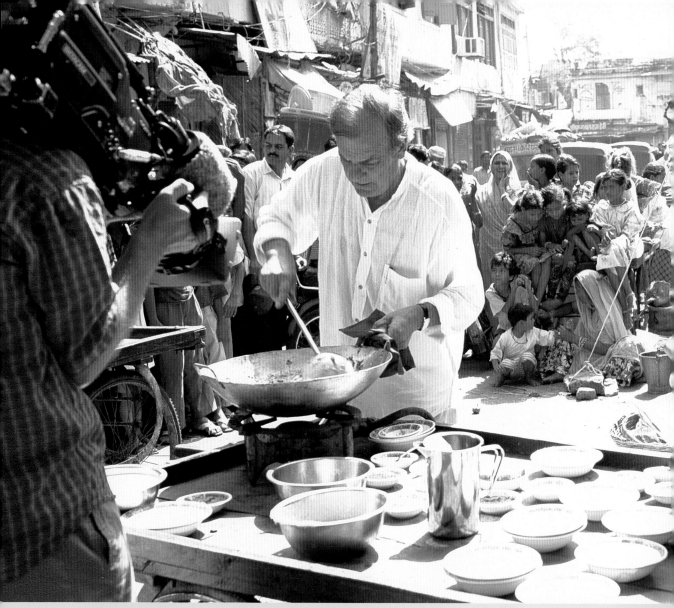

Chicken

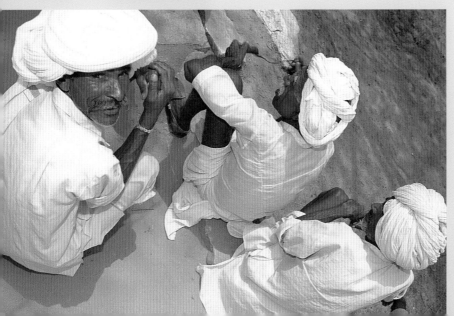

Chicken Dishes

Unless you happen to have a backyard full of very long-legged, thin, scrawny, bad-tempered chickens that eat nothing but what they can scavenge from the dustbins and scratch out of the earth with their very long-toed, hideous, gnarled feet, you are going to have difficulty in capturing the authentic flavour of an Indian chicken dish. The Indians do not have a squeamish and sanitised approach to food, unlike we Westerners who refuse to accept that chickens have bones, so, for a start, all the chicken used is cooked on the bone, the oldest and the toughest ones are chopped into bite-sized pieces (and that is the whole chicken, by the way, nothing is wasted) and are simmered slowly in fragrant and spicy sauces. Young, but equally scrawny chickens are preferred for grilling and roasting in the tandoor oven. So, if you can, try to find a source of fairly elderly free-range cockerels so that you can really enjoy the following recipes.

Below left to right *People of Jaipur, Rajasthan. Going shopping in Udaipur market.*

Chicken cafrael

This chicken in green masala has the quite enigmatic flavour that vinegar – in this case white wine vinegar – gives to Goan cooking. The chicken can be barbecued, shallow-fried or roasted in the oven. In my view shallow-fried is best because you can enjoy the juices from the pan. It is very nice served with a little onion and tomato salad. Incidentally, a legacy of the Portuguese occupation of Goa is that a lot of the dishes have English names.

serves 4

4 free-range chicken breasts

vegetable or coconut oil

salt

for the masala

2.5 cm/1 inch piece of root ginger, peeled and chopped

2 or 3 cloves of garlic, peeled

a handful of fresh coriander leaves with no stalks

1 teaspoon coriander seeds

1 teaspoon black peppercorns

3 or 4 cloves

4 cardamom pods

a small piece of cinnamon stick

4 or 5 fresh green chillies

white wine vinegar

1 Grind the masala ingredients, adding enough vinegar to make a dry but fairly smooth paste and season with salt.

2 Make several incisions in each chicken breast with a sharp knife and stuff with some of the masala, then coat the chicken pieces on both sides with the rest of the masala. Leave to marinate for about 1 hour.

3 Heat some oil in a pan and shallow-fry the chicken breasts gently on both sides until the chicken is cooked and the outside is crisp. Season with salt and serve with any residual pan juices. If you prefer to roast your chicken, drizzle a little oil over the masala-covered chicken breasts and roast until crisp in a hot oven; do the same thing if you are going to barbecue them.

Below *Mapusa market, Panjim, Goa.*

Above *Madras.*

Hot and dry chicken curry Kozhi masala fry

This is a Chettinad, a very hot and dry chicken curry that is typical of the Madras region.

serves 4–6

vegetable or coconut oil

2 cinnamon sticks

3 or 4 cloves

1 or 2 pieces of star anise

1 or 2 bay leaves

500 g/1 lb 2 oz red onions, finely chopped

250 g/9 oz tomatoes, chopped

1 kg/2¼ lb chicken pieces on the bone

salt

for the masala

1 tablespoon ground cumin

1 tablespoon ground fennel

1 tablespoon poppy seeds or small black
    mustard seeds

100 g/4 oz ginger and garlic purée (see
    page 56)

1 tablespoon ground turmeric

2 tablespoons red chilli powder

2 teaspoons ground coriander

1 Grind all the masala ingredients to a paste. Heat some oil, add the cinnamon sticks, cloves, star anise and bay leaves and fry until they crackle. Stir in the chopped onions and sauté until translucent, then add the tomatoes and cook until you have a rich tomato gravy.

2 Stir in the masala paste, adding a little water if it is too dry. Add the chicken pieces, season with salt, cover and cook slowly until the chicken pieces are done and are well coated with the gravy.

Above *Cooking in front of the splendid Victoria Monument, Calcutta.*

Duck curry Kosher hansher

The use of mustard seed oil and mustard seed paste is very dominant in Bengali cooking, and the oil certainly gives this curry a curious flavour. You must use it sparingly as I, for one, find it pungent and harsh. In fact, you may prefer to use a blander vegetable oil, but try both and make up your own mind.

serves 4

300 g/11 oz red onions, finely sliced

mustard seed oil

salt

1 duck, chopped, on the bone, into morsels

for the masala

about 10 g/⅓ oz garam masala (2 bay
   leaves, 6 cloves, broken stick of
   cinnamon, 6 or 8 cardamoms)

1 tablespoon ground coriander

1 tablespoon ground turmeric

2 tablespoons red chilli powder

2 tablespoons ginger and garlic purée
   (see page 56)

1 Sauté the sliced onions in mustard seed oil until they are brown but not burnt.

2 Then add the garam masala and fry until it crackles.

3 Stir in the coriander, turmeric and chilli powder, mix well and cook until the mixture is no longer powdery. Stir in the ginger and garlic purée and enough water to make a thick gravy. Season with salt.

4 Pop in the pieces of duck and simmer until tender.

Chicken curry Murgh masala

This is a terribly simple curry, much favoured by the Parsi community. For curry addicts in a hurry it is not only authentic, but quite quick. You can, of course, use mutton or lamb if you prefer.

serves 4

vegetable oil or ghee

2 red onions, finely sliced

4 or 5 red tomatoes, coarsely chopped

1 whole chicken, weighing about 1 kg/ 2¼ lb on the bone, chopped into morsels, or 500–600 g/1 lb 2 oz– 1¼ lb boneless chicken, cut into morsels (remember chicken on the bone will taste better but is more fiddly to eat)

salt

1 teaspoon brown sugar

small handful of chopped fresh coriander leaves

1 teaspoon garam masala (see page 61)

for the masala

1 or 2 green chillies, coarsely chopped

2 cloves of garlic, peeled and finely chopped

2.5 cm/1 inch piece of root ginger, peeled and finely chopped

½ teaspoon ground turmeric

½ teaspoon chilli powder

1 Mix all the masala ingredients together in a bowl without any liquid.

2 Heat the oil or ghee and sauté the onions until they are golden brown.

3 Stir in the tomatoes and cook gently until you have a rich onion and tomato gravy. Add the masala and stir well.

4 Stir in the chicken and cook gently until any liquid that comes from the meat is absorbed into the gravy. Continue cooking until the mixture is quite dry.

5 Season to taste with salt, add the sugar and cover the chicken with water. Bring to the boil, then simmer gently until the chicken is cooked and the oil floats to the top of the gravy.

6 Before serving, sprinkle the curry with the chopped coriander leaves and a good pinch of garam masala.

Below *Jagdish Mandir Temple, Udaipur.*

Above *The bustling streets of Bombay.*

Chicken with spinach Saag murgh

Pieces of chicken on the bone are cooked in a spicy spinach and tomato mixture to make a delicious curry.

serves 4

ghee

1 kg/2¼ lb spinach leaves, well washed and drained

1 kg/2¼ lb chicken morsels on the bone or 500 g/1 lb 2 oz chicken morsels, boned

salt and pepper

oil

4 tomatoes, finely chopped

1 cinnamon stick

2 bay leaves

for the masala

1 tablespoon ginger purée (see page 56)

1 tablespoon garlic purée (see page 56)

1 large red onion, puréed

2 teaspoons red chilli powder

1 teaspoon ground fenugreek

1 Grind together the masala ingredients with a little water to form a paste.

2 Heat some ghee in a pan and stir-fry the spinach until it is soft and cooked. Pop it into a blender and process to a purée.

3 In another pan, heat some more ghee and sauté the chicken pieces until they are golden. Season with salt and pepper and put to one side.

4 Heat some oil in a pan and cook the chopped tomatoes, cinnamon stick and bay leaves until they turn into a rich tomato sauce or purée. Stir in the masala and continue cooking for 3 or 4 minutes.

5 Now stir in the spinach purée and mix well. Add the chicken and any cooking juices from the pan. Cover the pan and simmer for about 15 minutes or until the chicken is cooked. If the gravy is too dry, stir in a little water.

Chicken curry with saffron Murgh kesari

This is a really rich and creamy saffron-flavoured chicken curry. Not a dish for the health conscious!

serves 4

1 kg/2¼ lb boneless chicken morsels
salt
lemon juice
100 g/4 oz unsalted cashew nuts
milk
225 g/8 oz red onions, peeled
ghee or butter
7.5 cm/3 inch cinnamon stick, broken
    into flakes
4 or 5 green cardamom pods, crushed
3 or 4 whole cloves
3 or 4 cloves of garlic, peeled and puréed
4 cm/1½ inch piece of root ginger,
    peeled and puréed
1 cup natural yoghurt, thoroughly
    whisked with 2 tablespoons cold water
    or, better still, whizzed up in the
    blender with 2 ice cubes
a very generous pinch of saffron threads
    (preferable to powder wherever
    possible)
½ cup double cream
chopped fresh coriander leaves,
    to garnish

1 Put the chicken in a dish, sprinkle with salt and lemon juice and leave to marinate for 1 hour. Meanwhile, put the cashew nuts in a bowl, pour in enough milk to cover and leave to soak for 1 hour, then transfer to a food processor or blender and purée.

2 Boil the onions until tender, drain and purée in a food processor or blender.

3 Heat some ghee or butter in a pan and sauté the cinnamon, cardamom pods and cloves for 1–2 minutes, then add the puréed garlic, ginger and onions and stir-fry until the onions turn slightly golden.

4 Reduce the heat and stir in the whipped or blended yoghurt and the saffron.

5 Add the chicken pieces and simmer gently for 5–10 minutes. Stir in the cashew nut purée and mix well. Continue cooking gently until the chicken is tender.

6 Stir in the double cream, garnish with chopped coriander leaves and serve.

Right *Martin wires me for sound while director Nick looks on.*

Above *Can't quite recall what I found so funny in Udaipur market.*

Chicken cooked with yoghurt Murgh ki kadhi

In the recipes that call for yoghurt, coconut cream or indeed cream, always add it over a low heat and continue cooking over a low heat so that it doesn't curdle. And of course yoghurt always makes a dish quite mild so you can offer your guests a little dish of chopped green chillies to spice it up if they so wish.

serves 4

vegetable oil
½ teaspoon mustard seeds
a pinch of fresh curry leaves
150 g/5 oz red onions, finely chopped
100 g/4 oz tomatoes, finely chopped
25 g/1 oz green chillies, chopped
10 g/⅓ oz chopped root ginger
1 teaspoon coriander seeds
1 teaspoon ground coriander
1 teaspoon red chilli powder
1 teaspoon ground turmeric
salt
500 g/1 lb 2 oz chicken morsels
2 whole red chillies
100 ml/4 fl oz natural yoghurt

1 Heat some oil in a *karai* or wok, add the mustard seeds and curry leaves and fry until they crackle. Add the onions, tomatoes, green chillies and ginger and cook until you have a thick gravy.

2 Stir in the coriander seeds, ground coriander, red chilli powder, turmeric and salt to taste.

3 Add the chicken pieces and red chillies and cook, stirring all the while, until the gravy has reduced and the oil has separated.

4 Lower the heat, stir in the yoghurt and cook gently until the chicken is completely cooked.

Chicken with tomato gravy Murgh tikka makhani

In this dish chicken is cooked in a rich tomato gravy scented with fenugreek leaves.

serves 6

vegetable oil

4 or 5 cloves of garlic, peeled and finely
  chopped

800 g/1¾ lb chicken morsels

2 or 3 tablespoons fenugreek leaves

salt and pepper

150 ml/5 fl oz double cream

2 tablespoons ghee

3 tablespoons honey

for the tomato gravy

1 kg/2¼ lb whole tomatoes

3 or 4 small red onions, peeled

4 or 5 cloves of garlic, peeled

5 cm/2 inch piece of root ginger, peeled
  and chopped

5 or 6 fresh green chillies

5 green cardamom pods

1 teaspoon ground coriander

1 teaspoon ground cinnamon

½ teaspoon ground mace

3 or 4 cloves

1 Put all the ingredients for the tomato gravy in a pan with a little water, bring to the boil and cook for a few minutes. Cool slightly, then purée in a food processor or blender to make a smooth red gravy.

2 Heat some oil and fry the chopped garlic until brown. Add the chicken pieces and stir-fry until they are golden.

3 Pour in the tomato gravy and simmer gently until the chicken is almost cooked. Stir in the fenugreek leaves and season with salt and pepper.

4 Just before serving, stir in the cream, the ghee and the honey.

Tandoori

Above left to right *Making tandoori kebabs; a newly made tandoor oven, Amritsar; lighting the fire.*

Tandoori Dishes

There is no mystique to a tandoor oven. It is simply a conical tube of sun-baked clay with a wood or charcoal fire laid at the bottom and with an air vent at ground level. The idea is that, because of its shape, there is first the heat from below and then reflected heat that comes from the internal wall of the oven. Food to be cooked is threaded on to a long skewer and placed upright in the tube. You will get exactly the same effect from a wood-fired pizza oven and you can achieve a similar effect by grilling tandoori dishes over a charcoal barbecue. You can, of course, make the following dishes taste quite good in an ordinary oven but, without doubt, cooking tandoori recipes over wood or charcoal in an enclosed clay or brick oven will give you the very best results.

If you actually own a tandoor oven, you will know that you have to invert the large laden skewers vertically in your tandoor. Gravity dictates that the food will slide down the skewer if you do not take certain measures to avoid this. The best solution is to impale a raw potato on to the very end of the skewer (nearest the fire) to stop the food sliding down. When your food is cooked, discard the potato as it will be burnt beyond recognition.

Now if you fancy a trip to Amritsar in the Punjab you can stroll down Tandoori Alley and have a tandoor custom built. The lady will mix clay with water and coconut fibre and over a couple of days handcraft you a tandoor to your specifications.

While you're waiting I suggest you stay with my friend Sanjay in the M.K. Hotel for a couple of days while the oven is sundried before it is cured inside with a mixture of mustard oil, jaggery (sugar), yoghurt and ground spinach. In July 2001 I purchased for about 70 pence a tandoor oven that stood 3 feet high. Unfortunately British Airways wanted, in my opinion, an absolutely outrageous sum of money per kilo to fly it back to the UK and it would have cost about £600 in excess baggage so sadly it stayed put in India. After this experience the film crew and I changed our airline to Emirates, who were pleased to have our business and our filming equipment.

Classically, tandoori dishes are served with some very, very thin fresh, raw red onion rings, a wedge of lime, thin slices of cucumber and tomato, and mint and coriander chutney (see page 173).

Tandoori chicken

Probably the most popular tandoori dish is tandoori chicken. The secret of its success lies in the marinade and in the quality of the chicken used. It really is important to use a genuine free-range bird that has also got a bit of experience. By this I mean a bit of a tough old bird! This version of the traditional dish is adapted for cooking in a domestic oven.

Serves 4–6

1 chicken, cleaned and skinned
vegetable oil for basting

for the chilli marinade

2 teaspoons red chilli powder
a big pinch of salt
lemon juice

for the creamy marinade

1 teaspoon ground cumin
1 teaspoon garlic purée (see page 56)
1 teaspoon ginger purée (see page 56)
a pinch of saffron threads
about 1 cup cream
about 1 cup yoghurt

Note

You can do exactly the same thing with large, shelled, de-veined (just remove the thin intestinal vein that runs down the back of each prawn) prawns or with fillets of skinned and boned fish. If using prawns – and they must be large – run a knife down the back of the prawn so that they will open up like butterflies as they cook.

1 Score the chicken on the breast, thighs and legs. Mix together the ingredients for the chilli marinade, adding enough lemon juice to make a paste to rub all over the chicken, inside and out. Smear it over the chicken and leave for 30 minutes.

2 Whisk all the ingredients for the creamy marinade into a thick paste and liberally smear the marinade over the chicken, inside and out. Allow to marinate in the fridge for at least 3 hours.

3 Place the bird on a roasting rack with the tray underneath to catch any drips and bake in the oven preheated to 130°C/250°F/Gas Mark ¼ for about 20 minutes and then whack up the heat to at least 180°C/350°F/Gas Mark 4 and cook until the bird is almost ready.

4 Baste with oil and cook for a further couple of minutes. Common sense needs to be applied here. That is to say, the chicken should be slightly crispy or even a little bit burnt on the outside but moist and tender on the inside.

Tandoori prawns Tandoori jhinga

It is essential that you have very large raw prawns for this dish. They can be
threaded on to skewers or laid straight on the barbecue grill or on a grill pan.

per person

as many large prawns per person as you
 feel like paying for
melted butter or ghee
lemon juice
1 teaspoon chaat masala (see page 61)

**for the marinade (enough for about
a dozen prawns)**

6 teaspoons ginger and garlic purée (see
 page 56)
juice of 1 lemon or lime
3 teaspoons gram flour (chickpea flour)
1 teaspoon garam masala (see page 61)
1 teaspoon red or yellow chilli powder
½ teaspoon ground turmeric
salt
2 cups natural yoghurt

1 Remove the head and the shell from each prawn but
leave the tail on. Run a knife down the back of the prawn
and remove the thin black intestinal vein. Flatten each
prawn very slightly.

2 Whisk together the marinade ingredients. Smear the
prawns with the marinade and leave them for 2 hours.

3 Preheat the grill, barbecue or tandoor oven. Thread
the prawns on to skewers, if using, and cook for about
10 minutes.

4 Remove the prawns from the heat and baste with
butter or ghee and lemon juice. Sprinkle with chaat
masala and return to the heat just to finish them off.

Minced lamb kebabs

This is a really exotic kebab. Indeed it is the maharajah of kebabs. A common version of this dish would probably just be minced lamb, a bit of mint, bit of green chilli, bit of coriander and a bit of garlic slapped on a skewer. This one, however, is rather special with a long list of tempering – that is to say flavouring or seasoning – ingredients. If you cannot get some of them, do not be discouraged, just leave them out and do the best you can.

makes about 20

500 g/1 lb 2 oz minced lamb
oil for basting

for tempering

3 teaspoons ginger purée (see page 56)
3 teaspoons garlic purée (see page 56)
3 tablespoons brown onion paste (see page 56)
1 tablespoon grated fresh coconut
2 tablespoons natural yoghurt
2 tablespoons cream
2 teaspoons freshly ground black pepper
½ teaspoon ground cinnamon
½ teaspoon ground cloves
1 teaspoon cumin seeds
¼ teaspoon ground black cardamom (if possible)
½ teaspoon ground mace
1 teaspoon crushed poppy seeds (if possible)
1 teaspoon red chilli powder
3 tablespoons gram flour (chickpea flour)
1 tablespoon finely chopped fresh mint leaves
1 tablespoon finely chopped fresh coriander leaves
1 teaspoon ground papaya (if possible)
salt and pepper to taste

1 Mix the whole lot together. Dip your hands in cold water to enable you to mould the mixture into thin sausages about 12.5 cm/5 inches long.

2 Preheat the grill, barbecue or tandoor oven. Squeeze the sausages tightly on to a skewer and cook until crispy on the outside and tender on the inside – about 10 minutes.

Opposite *Minced lamb kebabs and Tandoori-roasted stuffed peppers (page 107).*

Above *A colourful audience at Imely Pura, Udaipur.*

Vegetarian tandoori kebab

This is a kebab of vegetables, cheese and fruits, delightfully marinaded, which can be roasted in a tandoor or slightly charred over a charcoal barbecue or grill. Cut the ingredients into uniform, bite-sized pieces that will look attractive threaded on to a skewer. Increase the amount of marinade depending on the number of kebabs you are serving.

cubes of paneer (see page 183)
red or green peppers, deseeded and pith
    removed and cut into squares
peeled red onions, cut into wedges
tomatoes, cut into wedges
fresh pineapple or mango, cut into cubes

for the marinade
4 teaspoons garam masala (see page 61)
4 teaspoons chaat masala (see page 61)
juice of 2 or 3 lemons or limes
vegetable oil
salt

1 Mix together all the marinade ingredients and chuck in the cheese, vegetables and fruit. Leave to marinate for 2 hours.

2 Thread the fruit, vegetables and cheese on to the skewers in an attractive red, green and white sort of way and grill until tender and slightly browned.

Tandoori-roasted stuffed red or green peppers

Instead of large peppers you can use several little ones and make up the amount of filling to suit the size of the peppers you are using.

serves 4

4 red or green peppers of a uniform size
vegetable oil or ghee

for the masala

1 teaspoon cumin seeds
1 teaspoon garlic purée (see page 56)
1 teaspoon ginger purée (see page 56)
½ teaspoon garam masala (see page 61)
½ teaspoon red chilli powder
salt

for the stuffing

a selection of very finely chopped or
    shredded vegetables, such as green
    beans, carrots, white cabbage, onions,
    and peas (the quantities will depend
    upon the size or quantity of your
    peppers)
1 tablespoon crushed cashew nuts
1 tablespoon raisins or sultanas
1 tablespoon chopped fresh coriander
    leaves
1 cup of crumbled paneer (see
    page 183)

1 Slice the top off each pepper and reserve the top for a lid. Remove the pith and seeds.

2 Heat some oil or ghee, add the cumin seeds for the masala and fry until they crackle. Stir in the rest of the masala ingredients, adding salt to taste, and cook for a moment to release the flavours.

3 Add the vegetables for the stuffing and stir-fry until the oil separates. Remove from the heat and allow to cool.

4 Once the vegetables and masala are cool, add the cashew nuts, raisins or sultanas, coriander and cottage cheese.

5 Stuff the peppers with the mixture and replace the lids. Brush the peppers with oil and bake in a hot oven for about 15 minutes, depending on the size of the pepper. Alternatively, cook them under the grill or thread them on to skewers and place in a tandoor oven until the peppers are cooked.

Tandoori fish

Often in India a flat fish called pomfret is used for this dish, but you could use red mullet, bass, or indeed, any whole fish. In the event of a fish such as a bass or mullet, clean and de-scale the fish. I used pomfret here.

per person
1 fish
oil for basting

for the marinade (enough for 4 fish)
½ cup natural yoghurt
½ cup cream
2 teaspoons ground cumin
4 teaspoons garlic purée (see page 58)
4 teaspoons ginger purée (see page 58)
1 teaspoon ground turmeric
2 teaspoons red chilli powder
the juice of 1 or 2 lemons
a good pinch of salt
4 teaspoons gram flour (chickpea flour)
pepper

1 Cut 3 or 4 slashes on both sides of the fish.

2 Whisk together all the ingredients for the marinade to form a fairly thick paste. Smear the fish thoroughly, inside and out, with the marinade and leave to stand in the fridge for at least 2 hours.

3 If you happen to have a tandoor oven, skewer the fish from head to tail and cook in the oven for about 10 minutes. If not, heat the grill until it is very hot, place the fish on a rack and grill for about 10 minutes. Just before it is ready, baste with oil.

Below *Lakeside Palace, Udaipur.*

Fish

Above *Bombay duck drying on Gorai Beach, Bombay.*

Fish

As is common in most other countries, good fish and particularly shellfish are very expensive in India and most of the fish on sale in the smaller towns and villages is undersized and of poor quality. But nothing is wasted – fish heads are used for curries and where the fish are big enough to have backbones, they, as with lamb and chicken, are cooked on the bone.

One of the most popular fishes is called a pomfret. It is a flat fish and absolutely splendid for shallow frying, grilling or

barbecuing, and you will be able to find this in many cities in Britain these days. However, the choice of fish is a very personal thing so just because I recommend, for example, monkfish or bass, you can in fact substitute any fish that appeals to you.

Prawns in coconut milk Jhinga ularthiyathu

This is a fragrant, creamy, yet tangy, dish of prawns cooked in coconut milk. It is a relatively dry dish – the prawns should end up being coated in the sauce, rather than swimming in it.

serves 4

2 or 3 pieces of tamarind

1 kg /2¼ lb raw tiger prawns, shell on

juice of 3 limes

2 dessertspoons ground turmeric

salt

2.5 cm/1 inch piece of root ginger, peeled

3 or 4 cloves of garlic, peeled

coconut oil

200 g/7 oz small red shallots, coarsely chopped

2 teaspoons small black mustard seeds

a handful of fresh curry leaves

6 small tomatoes, cut into quarters with the seeds removed

½ cup slivers of fresh coconut

about 500 ml/18 fl oz coconut milk

for the masala

about 20 g/¾ oz chilli powder

about 15 g/½ oz ground coriander

1 teaspoon ground turmeric

1 teaspoon black pepper

about 10 g/⅓ oz ground cinnamon

about 10 g/⅓ oz ground cardamom

about 10 g/⅓ oz ground cloves

1 teaspoon ground fennel

1 Cover the pieces of tamarind with a little water, bring to the boil and simmer for 2 or 3 minutes, then set aside for 1 hour. Meanwhile, remove the head and shell from each prawn but leave the tail shell on. Cut down the back of each prawn so that they will open up like butterflies when cooked. With the point of the knife, remove the thin black intestinal vein that runs down the back of the prawns. Mix together the lime juice, turmeric and salt and marinate the prawns in this mixture in the fridge for 1 hour.

2 Mix together all the ingredients for the masala. Purée the ginger and the garlic in a food processor.

3 Heat some coconut oil in a pan and fry the shallots until soft. Add the mustard seeds and fry until they crackle, then stir in the powdered masala and cook gently for 2 or 3 minutes, until you have a nice smooth paste. Stir in the puréed ginger and garlic, then the curry leaves, tamarind and the tamarind-flavoured water. Add the tomatoes and coconut slivers and a little water, if necessary.

4 Add the prawns, then gently stir in the coconut milk and simmer for 3 or 4 minutes, until the prawns are cooked and the gravy is thickly coating the prawns. If you think the gravy is a little runny, remove the prawns and keep them warm. Reduce the gravy until it is thicker and then return the prawns to the pan.

Alleppey fish curry Macchi Alleppey

This is a creamy and spicy dish with an intriguing sourness created by slices of unripe mango. It comes from Alleppey, a coastal town in Kerala.

serves 4

1 large red onion, finely diced

coconut oil

2 small, unripe fresh mangoes, peeled and sliced

1 kg/2¼ lb firm fish fillets, such as monkfish, swordfish or large red snapper, cut into cubes

salt

for the masala

3 cups grated fresh coconut

25 g/1 oz chilli powder

10 g/⅓ oz ground turmeric

10 g/⅓ oz peeled and chopped root ginger

6 fresh green chillies, chopped

for the garnish

coconut oil

2 small red shallots, peeled and finely sliced

½ teaspoon small black mustard seeds

½ teaspoon fenugreek seeds

10–20 fresh curry leaves

1 Blend the masala ingredients to a smooth paste with a little water. Fry the diced red onion in some coconut oil until golden brown. Add the masala paste and a little water and cook over a low heat until you have a nice rich, creamy sauce. Add the sliced raw mangoes and cook for a couple of minutes until the mango slices have softened, then add the fish cubes, season with salt and simmer until the fish is cooked.

2 For the garnish, heat some coconut oil in a separate pan and stir-fry the shallots until softened. Add the mustard and fenugreek seeds and fry until they crackle, then quickly add the curry leaves and stir-fry until they are slightly crunchy and glistening. Sprinkle the garnish over the fish curry and serve.

Above *A lovely way to travel, aboard this splendid houseboat, on the Kerala backwaters.*

Fish in a banana leaf

Each fish is wrapped in a banana leaf to cook, sealing in all the flavour. If you can't find banana leaves, use large pieces of kitchen foil instead. I have no idea what the Indian name for this dish is – I devised it on a beautiful beach fringed with banana trees in Cochin.

serves 4

juice of 6 limes

10 g/⅓ oz ground turmeric

salt

4 small fish, such as mackerel, trout, or red mullet, weighing about 225 g/8 oz each, scaled, cleaned and de-finned (leave head and tail on)

coconut oil

4 small red onions, finely chopped

4 tomatoes, coarsely chopped

sprig of fresh curry leaves

2.5 cm/1 inch piece of root ginger, peeled and finely chopped

4 cloves of garlic, peeled and finely chopped

6 green chillies, coarsely chopped

20 g/¾ oz red chilli powder

4 banana leaves

chopped fresh coriander leaves

1 Mix together the lime juice, half the turmeric and some salt and marinate the fish in this mixture for 1 hour.

2 Heat some oil in a pan and sauté the onions until soft. Add the chopped tomatoes and cook until you have a rich tomato and onion sauce. Then add the curry leaves, ginger, garlic, green chillies, chilli powder and remaining turmeric and cook until no longer powdery. If necessary, add a little water and continue cooking until you have a thick gravy.

3 Meanwhile, heat some oil in a separate pan until very hot, then add the fish and sear on both sides so that the skin is crispy but the flesh is not cooked. Place each fish on a banana leaf and cover it with some of the gravy. Sprinkle some chopped coriander leaves on each portion, fold the banana leaf into a packet and bake for about 10 minutes in a hot oven.

Spicy fried fillets of fish Meen varuval

Any firm-fleshed fish, such as salmon, swordfish or monkfish, can be used for this dish but the fillets must come from a big fish.

serves 4–6

800 g/1¾ lb boned and skinned fillets of
    fish, cut into pieces about 7.5 cm/
    3 inches by 4 cm/1½ inches and
    12 mm/½ inch thick
juice of 2 lemons
salt
50 g/2 oz green chillies
50 g/2 oz red shallots or onion, chopped
50 g/2 oz root ginger, peeled and chopped
4 teaspoons white vinegar (rice vinegar
    would be good)
½ tablespoon ground turmeric
vegetable or coconut oil

1 Season the fish fillets with the lemon juice and some salt and set aside while you blend the chillies, shallots or onion, ginger, vinegar and turmeric to a thick paste, adding a drop of water if necessary.

2 Coat the fish fillets on both sides with this paste. In a frying pan, heat some oil and shallow-fry the fish until crispy on both sides.

Spicy prawns with mango Jhinga thokku

For this dish, prawns are quickly stir-fried with mangoes and spices for a stunning combination of flavours. You can use tiger or any large fresh prawns.

serves 4

500 g/1 lb 2 oz large raw prawns,
    shell on
200 g/7 oz red onions, finely sliced, or
    small red shallots, chopped
vegetable or coconut oil
1 tablespoon ground coriander
2 tablespoons red chilli powder
200 g/7 oz tomatoes, sliced
2 medium mangoes, peeled and diced
chopped fresh coriander leaves,
    to garnish

1 Remove the head and shell from each prawn. With the point of a knife, remove the thin black intestinal vein that runs down the back of the prawns.

2 Sauté the onions or shallots in some oil until translucent. Stir in the ground coriander and chilli powder and cook for 2 or 3 minutes.

3 Add the tomatoes and continue cooking until they have disintegrated and have amalgamated well with the spices and onions.

4 Stir in the diced mangoes and cook slowly until they have softened. Add the prawns and stir-fry for a minute or two, until cooked to your satisfaction. Garnish with chopped coriander leaves and serve.

Mackerel recheade

This is a typically Goan dish, distinguished by the vinegar-flavoured masala.
It is a perfect barbecue dish, but equally suitable for very shallow-frying. The
finished dish should have a crisp, crunchy skin. If you don't like mackerel, use
trout or red mullet.

serves 4

4 mackerel, cleaned, de-scaled and
   de-finned, with head and tail left on
salt
finely crushed black peppercorns
juice of 2 or 3 limes or lemons
a little plain flour
vegetable or coconut oil

for the masala

6 or 7 dried red chillies
1 teaspoon cumin seeds
5 or 6 cloves of garlic, peeled
1 tablespoon ground turmeric
1 teaspoon black peppercorns
2.5 cm/1 inch piece of root ginger,
   peeled
4 or 5 cardamom pods
1 small cinnamon stick
2 or 3 cloves
1 heaped tablespoon sugar
2 tablespoons tiny dried prawns
   (available from Asian food shops) or a
   dash of fish sauce
50 ml/2 fl oz red wine vinegar

1 Make 3 shallow incisions on either side of the fish with
a sharp knife. Season the fish inside and out with salt,
peppercorns and lime or lemon juice and marinate for
15 minutes or so.

2 Meanwhile, grind the masala ingredients to a fine
paste with the vinegar.

3 Apply the paste to the inside of the fish and into the
incisions on the outside.

4 If shallow-frying the fish, dredge them in a little flour
before cooking in a little oil; if you are barbecuing them,
paint the fish lightly with some oil and cook until tender.

Crab curry Kekada rasedaar

This delicious dish is messy because you have to crack the crab claws and eat with your fingers, but it is worth it! The stylish host would provide rosewater fingerbowls for the guests.

serves 4

vegetable or coconut oil

1 tablespoon small black mustard seeds

10–15 fresh curry leaves

100 g/4 oz red onion or red shallots, finely chopped

150 g/5 oz tomatoes, chopped

1 teaspoon ground turmeric

1 tablespoon red chilli powder

25 g/1 oz ginger and garlic purée (see page 56)

500 ml/18 fl oz coconut milk

salt

2 or 3 small raw crabs per person, chopped in half, cleaned out, gills and stomach sac removed and the claws cracked

a handful of small fresh curry leaves or fresh mint or coriander leaves, to garnish

1 Heat some oil in a pan, add the mustard seeds and curry leaves and cook until the mustard seeds crackle.

2 Stir in the onion or shallots and sauté until soft, then add the chopped tomatoes and cook until you have a rich tomato and onion gravy.

3 Stir in the turmeric and chilli powder and cook until the raw flavour disappears. Add a little water to help you do this, if necessary.

4 Now stir in the ginger and garlic purée and the coconut milk and simmer gently until you have a nicely amalgamated gravy. Season to taste with salt, then pop in the crabs and cook them gently until the shells have turned red.

5 If using curry leaves for the garnish, quickly stir-fry them in very hot oil and sprinkle them over the crabs. Alternatively scatter with fresh mint or coriander leaves and serve.

Below These are the sort of pots, pans and burners I cooked on during my trip. Here I'm cooking on a beach near Fisherman's Cove, Madras.

Mussels with green masala Thisra

Mussels are cooked in their shells in a herby green masala and coconut gravy. Make sure you buy fresh mussels and clean them thoroughly.

serves 4–6

1.5 kg/3¼ lb mussels (or as many as you want)

vegetable oil or coconut oil

2 red onions, finely diced

400 ml/14 fl oz can coconut milk

salt

for the masala

a very generous handful of fresh coriander leaves (no stalks)

a small handful of fresh mint leaves (no stalks)

1 cinnamon stick

6 cloves

10 or 12 black peppercorns

2.5 cm/1 inch piece of root ginger, peeled

2 cloves of garlic, peeled

1 teaspoon ground turmeric

5 or 6 fresh green chillies

2 tablespoons tamarind purée (see page 57)

1 Scrub the mussels under running water and debeard them. Then, with your forefinger and thumb, squeeze each shell sideways to try and open it. If the mussel doesn't budge, it means it is not filled with the fine mud that you occasionally find in a batch of mussels. Throw away any open mussels. Drain the mussels and keep cool.

2 Grind all the masala ingredients into a paste, adding a little water, if necessary.

3 Heat the oil in a pan and sauté the onions until they are soft. Stir in the masala and cook for a few moments, then add the coconut milk and cook for a little while until you have a delicious gravy. Season with salt.

4 Add the mussels to the pan and cook over a medium heat until the shells have opened. Discard any that don't open.

Below *More waterside cooking, this time in Goa.*

Dry clam curry

The masala in this curry and the green masala used in Mussels with green masala (see opposite) combine well with virtually any shellfish.

serves 4

3 small red onions, finely chopped
3 or 4 tomatoes, finely chopped
vegetable oil
3 or 4 green chillies, finely chopped
900 g–1.35 kg/2–3 lb good-sized clams
salt
chopped fresh coriander leaves, to
  garnish

for the masala

1 tablespoon ground turmeric
½ tablespoon finely crushed black
  peppercorns
2 cloves of garlic, peeled
2.5 cm/1 inch piece of root ginger,
  peeled
juice of 1 or 2 limes

1 Sauté the onions and tomatoes in the oil until you have a rich tomato sauce. Blend the masala ingredients to make a smooth paste.

2 Stir the green chillies into the tomato and onion sauce and cook for a short while. Add the masala and continue cooking until you have a rich, dryish gravy.

3 Add the clams and cook gently until they open. They should exude enough liquid to dampen the gravy; if not, add a little water. Season to taste with salt, garnish with the chopped coriander leaves and serve.

Below right *Before you can cook it, you've got to catch it.*

Above left to right *Cinnamon sticks; a Calcutta market; fish curry.*

Fish curry Bengal-style Doi macchi

Fish fillets are cooked in a spicy gravy that is cooled with natural yoghurt.

serves 4

mustard seed oil

4 bay leaves

2 cinnamon sticks

2 or 3 pieces of mace

4 or 5 whole cardamom pods

5 or 6 fresh green chillies, sliced

25 g/1 oz ground turmeric

10 g/$\frac{1}{3}$ oz ground coriander

250 g/9 oz red onion purée (see page 56)

15 g/$\frac{1}{2}$ oz ginger purée (see page 56)

300 ml/10 fl oz natural yoghurt

800 g/1$\frac{3}{4}$ lb skinned and boned firm
    fish fillets

salt

sugar

50 g/2 oz raisins or toasted nuts,
    to garnish

1 Heat some mustard seed oil in a pan, add the bay leaves, cinnamon, mace and cardamom pods and fry until they crackle.

2 Add the sliced chillies and stir-fry for a moment or two, then mix in the ground turmeric and coriander and fry for a few moments to cook the powder. Stir in the onion and ginger purées, mix well and then add enough water to make a smooth gravy.

3 Over a low heat, whisk in the yoghurt until you have a creamy gravy. Take care not to overheat the gravy or it will curdle. Pop in the fish pieces, season with a little salt and sugar and simmer gently until the fish is cooked. Garnish with the raisins or nuts and serve.

Above *A very busy street in Calcutta.*

Steamed fish fillets Paturi macchi

Fish fillets are coated in mustard paste and steamed in banana leaf parcels for a beautifully tender result. If you can't find banana leaves, use pieces of kitchen foil.

serves 4

800 g/1¾ lb boned and skinned fish
    fillets, cut into 10 cm/4 inch squares,
    about 12 mm/½ inch thick
banana leaves, cut into 20 x 12.5 cm/
    8 x 5 inch rectangles (one for each
    fish square)
salt

for the mustard paste

2 or 3 tablespoons yellow mustard seeds
2 teaspoons red chilli powder
2 teaspoons ground turmeric
1 tablespoon ginger and garlic purée (see
    page 56)
sugar to taste
mustard oil
6 fresh green chillies, chopped

1 Grind all the mustard paste ingredients, except the green chillies, adding just enough oil to make a paste. Then stir in the chopped chillies.

2 Season the fish with salt and then coat the fish squares on both sides with the mustard paste and wrap each one in a neat banana leaf parcel, and secure with a cocktail stick.

3 Heat the water in the base of a steamer to simmering point, put the fish in the steamer, cover with a tight-fitting lid and steam for 4–5 minutes, until cooked.

Chingri malai curry

Large prawns, such as tiger prawns, are cooked with cashew nuts and coconut milk.

serves 4

8 or 12 large raw prawns, shell on
vegetable oil
1 teaspoon cardamom pods
a couple of bay leaves
1 cinnamon stick
about half a 400 ml/14 fl oz can coconut
    milk
salt
142 ml/5 fl oz carton of single cream, if
    necessary

for the masala

2 teaspoons red chilli powder
½ cup unsalted, and if possible fresh,
    cashew nuts, puréed with a little oil
2 teaspoons ground turmeric
2 or 3 red onions, peeled, chopped,
    boiled and puréed
2.5 cm/1 inch piece root ginger and 3 or
    4 cloves of garlic, both peeled and
    ground to a paste

1 Remove the head and shell from each prawn, leaving the tail shell on. With the point of a knife, remove the thin black intestinal vein that runs down the back of the prawns.

2 Mix together all the masala ingredients. Heat some oil in a pan, add the cardamom pods, bay leaves and cinnamon stick and fry until they crackle, then stir in the masala and cook until well amalgamated with the oil.

3 Over a low heat, stir in the coconut milk and mix well. Check for seasoning – you may want to add some salt. If the gravy is thick, thin it with a little single cream, add the prawns and simmer very gently until the prawns are cooked.

Above *Muttukaddu, Madras – skill, balance and grace.*

Green fish curry Macchi kovalam

This fish curry from Madras has a subtle flavour and a fresh green colour.

serves 4

12 small whole red shallots
vegetable or coconut oil
100 g/4 oz red onion, finely chopped
100 g/4 oz tomatoes, finely chopped
25 g/1 oz ginger and garlic purée (see
    page 56)
salt
600 g/1 lb 5 oz boned and skinned fish
    chunks, such as bass, red mullet or
    bream

for the masala

50 g/2 oz fresh coconut
8–10 fresh green chillies, chopped
small handful of fresh coriander leaves
small handful of fresh mint leaves

1 To make the masala, put the coconut into a food processor and process to a purée. Add all the remaining masala ingredients, saving a few of the coriander and mint leaves for garnishing, and grind to a paste. Set aside.

2 Sauté the whole shallots in some oil until they crack open and are golden. Remove the shallots from the pan and put to one side. Heat some more oil and sauté the chopped onion until translucent. Add the tomatoes, then stir in the ginger and garlic purée, season with salt and cook until you have a rich tomato sauce.

3 Stir in the masala and, if it is too dry, add a little water. Cook the mixture until you have a rich gravy.

4 Add the fish and simmer gently until the fish is lightly cooked. At the last minute, pop in the precooked shallots. Chop the reserved mint and coriander leaves, scatter them over the fish and serve.

Goan lobster curry

This curry can be made with fish fillets instead of lobster or crayfish, if you prefer – use a couple of thick fillets of the fish of your choice, skinned and boned.

serves 2

vegetable or coconut oil

1 small red onion, finely chopped

2 or 3 fresh green chillies, chopped

400 ml/14 fl oz can coconut milk

salt

1 fresh lobster or crayfish, as big as you can afford, cut lengthways in half, the spinal cord and any gunge in the head removed

3 or 4 pieces of tamarind

for the masala

6 or 7 dried red chillies

pinch of cumin seeds

1 tablespoon ground turmeric

2 teaspoons coriander seeds

4 or 5 black peppercorns

2 cloves of garlic, peeled

2.5 cm/1 inch piece of root ginger, peeled

1 Grind together the masala ingredients with a little water to make a smooth paste.

2 Heat some oil and sauté the onion until transparent, then add the green chillies. Stir in the masala paste and cook until no longer powdery.

3 Add the coconut milk, season with salt if necessary, and cook for a few moments, until you have a smooth gravy. Add the lobster and the pieces of tamarind and continue cooking gently for 7 or 8 minutes, until the lobster is cooked.

Below An attentive audience at Betim, Goa.

Meat

Meat Dishes

The cow might be sacred in India – and they certainly are a damned nuisance, kipping in the middle of the road or plodding up and down the runway of some airport or blocking the sidewalk as they try to eat a poster off the wall – but it is not true that you cannot eat beef in India. Also, there is no shortage of pork, and in fact in Goa nearly all meat vindaloos are prepared with pork.

But far and away the most popular meat, and to my mind the tastiest, is lamb, although, of course, it is not lamb – it is

Above *Outdoor cooking at the Taj Malabar, Kerala.*

goat and truly delicious it is too. As with their chickens, the
Indians like to cook their meat on the bone, quite simply
because it brings much more flavour to the dishes.

In the recipes that follow, I would suggest that you use fresh
lamb for grilled, barbecued or roasted dishes and really try hard
to find some mature mutton for the curries.

Beef ularthiyathu

This is a dry curry inasmuch as the dish is cooked long enough for the meat to absorb all of the cooking liquor. It should still be moist and taste spicy and slightly sour.

serves 4

1 large red onion, finely diced

coconut oil (preferably)

1 kg/2¼ lb stewing beef, cut into
    bite-sized pieces

1 cup sliced fresh coconut

1 heaped tablespoon slivers of peeled
    root ginger

½ wineglass of red wine vinegar

a sprig of fresh curry leaves

for the masala

1 cinnamon stick

10 cloves

4 dessertspoons coriander seeds

½ teaspoon fenugreek seeds

½ teaspoon small black mustard seeds

½ teaspoon cumin seeds

1 dessertspoon ground turmeric

1 dessertspoon chopped fresh red chillies
    or 1 shallow dessertspoon chilli powder

1 teaspoon black peppercorns

1 teaspoon fennel seeds

for the garnish

3 or 4 small red shallots, peeled and
    coarsely chopped

½ teaspoon fenugreek seeds

½ teaspoon small black mustard seeds

a handful of fresh curry leaves

> **Note**
> In all recipes using curry
> leaves, kaffir lime leaves are
> an acceptable substitute.
> They can usually be found in
> the Thai section of specialist
> food shops.

1 Blend all the masala ingredients to a powder and tip into a convenient container.

2 Fry the finely diced red onion in some coconut oil until it is softened. Stir in the powdered masala, mixing well with the oil and onion, and cook over a low heat for a minute or two. Add the meat, coconut, ginger, vinegar and about 10 or 12 small curry leaves. Stir thoroughly so that the meat is completely coated with the masala mix.

3 Add enough water to just cover the meat, then simmer gently until the meat is tender and has absorbed the liquid but is still moist.

4 For the garnish, heat some coconut oil in a separate pan and rapidly fry the red shallots. Stir in the fenugreek and mustard seeds so that they crackle for a second, then quickly add the curry leaves and stir-fry until they are slightly crunchy, dark green and glistening, but not burnt. Sprinkle the lot over the beef and serve.

Goan beef vindaloo

For those of us bought up on the ubiquitous Anglo-Indian beef vindaloo – that fiery, brown, sometimes red thing, washed down with copious amounts of lager – the Goan version is an enchanting discovery. It takes its name from the Portuguese intervention in Goan cooking, *Vin* (literally wine or vinegar in Portuguese) and *Aloo* (the Indian for potato), and it is the easiest thing in the world to cook!

serves 4

2 red onions, finely chopped

vegetable or coconut oil

about 800 g/1¾ lb diced beef (or pork; or large prawns, shelled and deveined; or, if using lamb or chicken, it is better on the bone; if you would like a vegetarian vindaloo, scrap all the above and just use potatoes!)

3 or 4 medium potatoes, peeled and cut into fairly large cubes

sugar

salt

for the masala

about 15 dried red chillies

4 fresh green chillies

a big piece of root ginger, peeled

1 teaspoon cumin seeds

1 teaspoon black peppercorns

1 teaspoon ground turmeric

3 or 4 cloves

2 cinnamon sticks

red wine vinegar

1 Blend all the masala ingredients, adding enough vinegar to make a smooth paste.

2 Sauté the onions in the oil until softened. Stir in the masala and cook for a few moments.

3 Stir in the meat (or prawns) and continue to cook for a few minutes until the meat and the masala have amalgamated. Add sufficient water to make a rich, fairly thick gravy and simmer gently until the meat is about half cooked.

4 Add the potato cubes and season with a little sugar and salt and continue cooking until the meat is tender and the potatoes are cooked. The gravy should be a natural, rich red colour, although in some parts of the world vindaloos are, quite improperly, artificially coloured, as indeed are many tandooris.

Mutton stew

Highly spiced mutton and potatoes are simmered in coconut milk for this stew. It is important that the coconut milk for the marinade is diluted – one part coconut milk to two parts water. The meat is brought to the boil and if you used thick coconut milk it would curdle and separate.

serves 4–6

two 400 ml/14 fl oz cans coconut milk

1 kg/2 ¼ lb mutton or lamb, cut into
  bite-sized cubes

coconut oil

about 150 g/5 oz small red shallots,
  coarsely chopped

1 teaspoon small black mustard seeds

4 or 5 fresh green chillies, chopped

1 dessertspoon puréed fresh garlic

1 dessertspoon puréed root ginger

1 sprig of fresh curry leaves

200 g/7 oz peeled potatoes, cut into
  bite-sized pieces

2 dessertspoons whole garam masala
  (this will be about 6 or 7 cardamom
  pods, ½ cinnamon stick, 6 or 7
  cloves, and 2 or 3 bay leaves)

salt

for the masala

1 teaspoon ground cumin

2 teaspoons ground coriander

2 teaspoons chilli powder

1 Mix half a can of coconut milk with twice that quantity of water to thin it and then marinate the cubed mutton or lamb in it for about 2 hours in the fridge.

2 Mix together the masala ingredients. Heat some coconut oil and fry the chopped shallots until golden. Add the mustard seeds and fry until they crackle, then add the green chillies. Stir in the puréed garlic and ginger and the curry leaves, then mix in the masala and sauté until you have a rich paste.

3 Now stir in the marinated mutton so that it is completely covered by the other ingredients in the pan. Add the whole garam masala. Tip in the watered-down coconut milk marinade and bring to the boil. Simmer for about 20 minutes, then add the potato chunks and season with salt. From time to time, as the liquid in the pan reduces, gradually add the remaining coconut milk until you have a thick, rich gravy and the mutton and the potatoes are tender.

Right *With Rasheed at the Taj Malabar, Kerala.*

Lamb dhansak

This is a substantial dish, much favoured by the Parsis, who are great meat eaters. It is a one-pot dish, often served for Sunday family lunch, and is generally served with brown rice, lemon wedges and an onion, tomato and cucumber relish called Kachumber (see page 176). Although this is traditionally a lamb or mutton dish, you could also use chicken.

serves 4–6

500 g/1 lb 2 oz yellow lentils, soaked overnight

100 g/4 oz red lentils, soaked overnight

100 g/4 oz mung peas, soaked overnight

oil or ghee

2 red onions, finely sliced

½ teaspoon ground turmeric

1 teaspoon ground coriander

1 teaspoon ground cumin

500 g/1 lb 2 oz stewing lamb or mutton, cut into cubes

1 aubergine, peeled and diced

250 g/9 oz pumpkin, peeled and diced

salt

500 g/1 lb 2 oz fresh spinach leaves, well washed and drained

for the masala

6–8 cloves of garlic, peeled

5 cm/2 inch piece of root ginger, peeled and chopped

6–8 dried red chillies

6 green cardamom pods

5 cm/2 inch piece of cinammon stick

½ teaspoon black peppercorns

1 tablespoon coriander seeds

1 tablespoon cumin seeds

1 Drain and rinse the lentils and mung peas. Grind together the masala ingredients with a little water to make a smooth paste.

2 Heat the oil or ghee and fry the onions until they are golden brown, then stir in the masala, the turmeric, coriander and cumin and stir-fry gently for about 5 minutes.

3 Over a low heat, stir in the lamb and cook gently until the meat is completely coated with the masala, and any liquid that has come from the meat has been absorbed into the masala. At this stage the dish should be quite dry.

4 Now add the lentils and peas, aubergine and pumpkin. Stir in a little water to form the basic gravy and season with salt. Bring to the boil, then reduce the heat, cover and simmer gently until the meat is cooked.

5 Remove the meat from the pan and put to one side. Purée the lentils, vegetables and gravy in a food processor and return the meat to this mixture.

6 Quickly stir-fry the spinach in hot oil and then add the spinach to the dish.

Opposite *Cooking with the Chef at the Taj Mahal Hotel, Bombay.*

Above *With Sandhu, Chef at the Trident Hotel in Jaipur.*

Lamb in fragrant brown gravy Nallie ke kaliyan

This delicious dish of lamb simmered in a mildly spiced but fragrant brown gravy was prepared for me by my friend Sandhu, who is the executive chef of the charming Trident Hotel in Jaipur. In this masala the spices are whole, not ground.

serves 4

500 g/1 lb 2 oz lamb or mutton, cut into
   bite-sized morsels
60 g/2 ½ oz mixed ginger and garlic purée
   (see page 56)
salt
vegetable oil
150 g/5 oz finely diced red onions
½ teaspoon ground turmeric
½ teaspoon chilli powder
1 teaspoon ground coriander
150 ml/5 fl oz tomato purée
50 ml/ 2 fl oz cream
toasted flaked almonds, to garnish (optional)

for the masala

2 blades of mace
10 green cardamom pods
4 black cardamom pods
10 cloves
3 bay leaves

1 Coat the lamb with half of the ginger and garlic purée seasoned to taste with salt, spreading it on with your fingers. Leave to marinate for at least 1 hour.

2 Heat some oil and fry the masala spices until they crackle. Add the diced onions and stir-fry until they are golden.

3 Add the remainder of the ginger and garlic purée with the ground spices. Season with salt. Stir in the lamb pieces and cook until the oil starts to separate. Now add a little water and simmer the lamb until it is tender.

4 Remove the lamb from the gravy and put to one side. Tip the gravy into a food processor and purée it. Strain the gravy, then gently reheat it in a pan. Add the tomato purée and simmer until you have a rich, thick sauce. Over a low heat, stir in the cream, and pop the meat back in the pan to warm through in the gravy. Garnish with the almonds, if using, and serve.

Mutton curry Laal maas

This is a very simple mutton, goat or lamb curry, which was originally prepared by the nomadic tribesmen when they made camp and was cooked gently over a wood fire.

serves 4–6

1 kg/2 ¼ lb stewing mutton or lamb, cut
    into bite-sized morsels
vegetable oil
3 or 4 red onions, finely chopped
150 g/5 oz natural yoghurt
salt

for the marinade

about 150 g/5 oz ginger and garlic purée
    (see page 56)
150 g/5 oz red chilli purée (you can grind
    dried red chillies with a little oil or
    make a paste with red chilli powder
    and a little oil)
400 g/14 oz natural yoghurt

for the garam masala

2 or 3 dried bay leaves
3 or 4 pieces of dried mace
5 or 6 green cardamom pods
1 cinnamon stick, broken into pieces
4 or 5 cloves

for the garnish

1 heaped tablespoon ghee or butter
1 heaped tablespoon chopped fresh
    coriander leaves

1 Mix together all the marinade ingredients. Add the lamb pieces and stir to coat with the marinade. Leave to marinate in the fridge for 2 hours.

2 Heat some oil and fry the onions until they are golden brown, then add all the garam masala ingredients and stir-fry for a few seconds.

3 Remove the lamb from the marinade and add it to the pan of onions. Sauté gently for 10–12 minutes, until the meat is quite dry and the oil has separated from the meat.

4 Add some water to form the gravy and simmer gently until you have a rich, red sauce and the lamb is cooked. At this stage, stir in the yoghurt, season with salt and cook for another 2 or 3 minutes, mixing well.

5 Just before serving, stir in the ghee or butter and the chopped coriander leaves.

*Opposite Around India in 100 Dishes,
helped by the indispensable Murry.*

Rogan josh

Lamb or mutton is simmered in a smooth gravy that is enriched with ground almonds.

serves 4

vegetable oil, for frying

800 g/1¾ lb lamb or mutton, cut into
   bite-sized morsels

1 cup yoghurt

salt

½ cup tomato purée

1 tablespoon ground almonds

for the masala

4 or 5 whole cardamom pods

3 or 4 cloves

4 tablespoons ginger and garlic purée
   (see page 56)

1 teaspoon chilli powder

2 tablespoons brown onion paste (see
   page 56)

½ tablespoon garam masala (see
   page 61)

for the garnish

chopped fresh coriander leaves

a piece of root ginger, peeled and cut into
   very thin sticks (julienne)

a big pinch of saffron threads soaked in
   3 tablespoons rosewater

1 To make the masala, heat some oil, add the cardamom pods and cloves and fry until they crackle. Add the rest of the masala ingredients and stir-fry for a minute or two.

2 Stir in the lamb and the yoghurt, season with salt and stir-fry for 3 or 4 minutes so that the meat is well covered with the masala and yoghurt. Add a little water and simmer gently until the lamb is almost tender.

3 Mix in the tomato purée and continue cooking until you have reduced the liquid by about one third. Stir in the ground almonds.

4 Finally, garnish with chopped coriander leaves and the ginger julienne, sprinkle the saffron and rosewater over the top and serve.

Marinated baked rabbit Khad khargosh

I cooked this excellent dish in an isolated Indian village 80 km/50 miles from Jaipur. Since simple Indian villages like the one I was visiting have no ovens, when they wish to bake or roast something they dig a small hole in the ground within the village compound and line it with dried cow dung, which whilst wet has been moulded into thick disks about 15 or 18 cm/6 or 7 inches in diameter and sun-dried. The cow dung is then ignited and once it is well alight, rather like charcoal, the rabbit is wrapped in many layers of banana leaves and covered with more cow dung disks. If you have no garden or if you live in a flat and can't dig a hole in the lawn, or indeed if you don't own a cow, simply wrap the prepared rabbit in kitchen foil and bake it in the oven.

serves 4–6
1 whole rabbit

for the marinade
25 g/1 oz mixed ginger and garlic purée (see page 56)
2 pinches of garam masala (see page 61)
juice of 3 or 4 limes
a little red chilli powder
salt

for the stuffing
100 g/4 oz cashew nuts, roughly crushed
100 g/4 oz sultanas

1 Mix the marinade ingredients to a smooth paste and apply it evenly all over the rabbit. Leave to marinate for 4–6 hours in the fridge.

2 Stuff the rabbit with the nuts and sultanas and sew up the cavity with some twine. Check that the rabbit is well coated with marinade on all sides. Wrap it in a large piece of kitchen foil and bake in a moderately hot oven for about an hour.

Note
A whole chicken can be cooked this way as well.

Vegetables

Vegetable Dishes

It is true to say that over the years I have scoffed at and poked
fun at vegetarians, quite unfairly, of course. But we all have
prejudices, however ill founded, and certainly as a man who
likes his steak bloody and lamb pink, and can feast on marrow
bones and pigs' trotters, a roasted pig's head, brains, tongue
and all, and as one who is never happier than when offered a
mountain of raspberries topped with crusty, thick, yellow
clotted cream, I am hardly the one to embrace the vegetarian
cause. But my visit to India has changed all that. Eating

vegetarian food in India is a wonderful experience. There are hundreds and hundreds of different dishes using every vegetable, pulse and grain known to man, from baby aubergines to lentils and sweetcorn, from string beans to potatoes, marrows, courgettes, pumpkins, onions and beetroot, all subtly and flavoursomely prepared. Indeed for a whole month on one of my trips to India I ate nothing but exquisite vegetable dishes. Didn't stop me from still enjoying my wine, of course. Anyway, the recipes that follow are a few of my personal favourites.

Okra sautéed with coconut Vendakai poriyal

This is a really refreshing way to enjoy okra (ladies' fingers) – they will not be glutenous because they are cooked so quickly.

serves 4

500 g/1 lb 2 oz okra, stems removed
coconut oil
2 teaspoons black mustard seeds
a handful of fresh curry leaves
2.5 cm/1 inch piece of root ginger,
    peeled and cut into thin strips
salt

for the masala

2 cups grated fresh coconut
5 or 6 fresh green chillies
1 heaped teaspoon cumin seeds
3 or 4 cloves of garlic, peeled

for the garnish

a handful of fresh curry leaves
coconut oil

1 Blend the masala ingredients to a paste. Cut the okra into small roundels.

2 In a pan, heat some coconut oil and fry the mustard seeds and curry leaves until they crackle, then add the ginger and quickly stir-fry.

3 Add a little more oil to the pan and when it is hot, add the okra and stir-fry until *al dente*. Stir in the masala paste and sauté for about 4 minutes, until all the pieces of okra are coated with the masala. The dish should be slightly crunchy. Check for seasoning and add some salt if necessary.

4 To make the garnish, quickly stir-fry the curry leaves in some hot coconut oil in a separate pan. Scatter them over the okra and serve.

Spiced beetroot Subzi poriyal

I am a confirmed beetroot eater, whether it is roasted or pickled in vinegar, and I was delighted to discover this crunchy, spicy, tangy dish in Madras. Serve it either as a starter or as an accompaniment.

serves 4–6

about 800 g/1¾ lb fresh beetroot, boiled
   in their skins in salted water and left
   to cool
100 ml/4 fl oz coconut or vegetable oil
   (coconut for preference)
1 heaped tablespoon black mustard seeds
150 g/5 oz red shallots or red onions,
   finely chopped
6 or 8 fresh green chillies, finely chopped
   (the more seeds you leave in, the
   hotter the dish, it is up to you)
150 g/5 oz grated fresh coconut
salt and pepper

1 Peel the cooked beetroot and chop into small cubes.

2 Heat the oil, add the mustard seeds and fry until they crackle. Stir in the shallots or onions and the green chillies and sauté for 2 or 3 minutes.

3 Add the grated coconut and stir-fry until it is slightly brown and toasted. Stir in the beetroot and mix well with the other ingredients, season with salt and pepper and serve.

Spicy vegetable curry Avial

For this spicy vegetable curry, cooked with fruit and coconut, you need a good selection of interesting vegetables, such as the ones suggested below.

serves 4

for the vegetables and fruit

(all ingredients are approximate and you can use any vegetables and fruit you like from an Asian shop, but about 100 g/4 oz of each of the following, cut into thick julienne strips, would be great)

yam

green bananas

green beans

white pumpkin

1 large unripe mango

3 dessertspoons ground turmeric

salt

for the masala

2 cups grated fresh coconut (or you could use dried)

5 or 6 fresh green chillies

1 teaspoon cumin seeds

6 or 8 very small red shallots, roughly chopped

6 fresh curry leaves

for the garnish

a handful of small fresh curry leaves

coconut oil

1 Grind the masala ingredients to a paste, adding a little water if necessary.

2 Put all the vegetables and fruit into a large pan and add just enough water to enable you to boil them. Stir in the turmeric, season with salt, then bring to the boil and cook until the vegetables are *al dente*. Drain off the turmeric-flavoured water and keep it handy in a jug.

3 Stir the masala into the vegetables and add sufficient turmeric-flavoured water to form a thick gravy. Continue cooking until the gravy has become creamy and spicy.

4 At the last moment, quickly stir-fry the curry leaves in some very hot coconut oil and then sprinkle them over the vegetables.

Opposite A Calcutta vegetable vendor (top). At a market in Madras (bottom).

Kathirikai kara kulambu Sweet and sour aubergines

This is a stunning dish of creamy baby aubergines cooked in a rich, spicy tomato and onion gravy. Try and use aubergines that are all the same size.

serves 4

vegetable or coconut oil

3 red onions, finely sliced

4 tomatoes, coarsely chopped

15–20 fresh curry leaves

500 g/1 lb 2 oz baby aubergines, stalks
    removed and cut in half lengthways

200 g/7 oz grated fresh coconut

2 tablespoons chilli powder

2 tablespoons ground coriander

2 teaspoons ground turmeric

200 g/7 oz tamarind purée (see page 57)

salt

chopped fresh coriander leaves, to
    garnish

1 Heat some oil and sauté the onions until they are completely soft. Add the tomatoes and continue cooking until you have a thick, rich onion and tomato gravy. You can add a little water, but be sure to cook until the water evaporates, leaving a thick, red gravy. Stir in the curry leaves.

2 While the tomato gravy is thickening, shallow-fry the aubergines in some oil in a separate pan until they are half-cooked, then put to one side.

3 Blend the coconut to a paste in a food processor, adding a little water if necessary. Mix together the powdered spices, the tamarind and the coconut paste and stir into the tomato and onion gravy. Season with salt.

4 Cook for 2 or 3 minutes, mixing well, then add the parcooked aubergines and simmer gently for about 20 minutes. Garnish with the chopped fresh coriander leaves and serve.

Yam fry Arbi pakode

Thin shavings of slightly sweet, parboiled yam are given a spicy coating and then shallow-fried until crispy.

500 g/1 lb 2 oz yam, peeled
salt
10 cloves of garlic, peeled
1 tablespoon fennel seeds
1 tablespoonful ground turmeric
2 tablespoons red chilli powder
vegetable or coconut oil
wedges of lime or lemon, to serve

1 Cut the yam into rectangles about 4 cm/1½ inches by 2.5 cm/1 inch and about 6 mm/¼ inch thick and cook in boiling salted water until they are *al dente*.

2 Purée the garlic and the fennel seeds in a blender, then add the turmeric and chilli powder and a drop of water to make a thick paste. Season with a little salt.

3 Drain the yam pieces and pat dry, then coat them on both sides with the paste. Heat some oil and shallow-fry the pieces on both sides until the paste is crispy but not burnt. Serve with wedges of lime or lemon.

Above *There is a stunning variety of vegetables and fruit at the market in Panjim, Goa.*

Runner or green beans foogath

This is simple, quick Indian cooking at its best – a tasty dish that enables you to enjoy spicy, crunchy green beans that have not had the goodness boiled out of them in gallons of salted water. It should be awarded two yum yums!

serves 4

vegetable or coconut oil

20 g/¾ oz cumin seeds

300 g/11 oz new potatoes, scrubbed and diced into 12 mm/½ inch cubes (maximum)

2 red onions, finely chopped

1 kg/2¼ lb french beans, topped and tailed or, if you are lucky enough to get them, fresh runner beans, stringed, topped and tailed and chopped into pieces about 12 mm/½ inch long (maximum)

6 dried red chillies, coarsely chopped

salt

1 teaspoon freshly ground black pepper

2 cups grated fresh coconut (dried coconut will not do in this instance)

1 Heat some oil in a pan, add the cumin seeds and cook until they crackle.

2 Add the potato cubes and onions and stir-fry until they are slightly colouring, then add just a tiny drop of water and cook until the water has evaporated and the potatoes are *al dente*.

3 Stir in the chopped beans without adding any more water, then stir in the chopped dried chillies and season with salt and pepper. Cook until the beans are tender, stirring all the while. Tip on to a serving dish and sprinkle with the grated fresh coconut.

Above *I cooked this dish on Gorai beach, Bombay.*

Spicy green tomatoes

serves 4

vegetable oil

½ teaspoon cumin seeds

½ teaspoon fenugreek seeds

500 g/1 lb 2 oz firm, green tomatoes, cut
   into quarters

2 or 3 fresh green chillies, coarsely
   chopped

salt

for the masala

1 teaspoon red chilli powder

2 teaspoons ground coriander

½ teaspoon ground turmeric

1 heaped teaspoon garlic purée (see
   page 56)

1 teaspoon sugar

1 Mix together all the masala ingredients with a little water to form a very dry paste.

2 Heat the oil and fry the cumin and fenugreek seeds until they crackle. Stir in the masala and cook for 2 or 3 minutes, then add the tomatoes and chillies. Season to taste with salt. Mix well together and cook gently until the tomatoes start to soften.

Stir-fried mustard greens and spinach

Although mustard greens are quite bitter, they are like that rare British delicacy purple sprouting broccoli, very tasty and very nutritious. You could, in fact, substitute young purple sprouting for mustard greens if you can get it.

serves 6

150 g/5 oz ghee

6 green chillies, cut in half lengthways and deseeded

5 cm/2 inch piece of root ginger, peeled and very finely chopped

1 kg/2 ¼ lb mustard greens, stalks removed and coarsely chopped

500 g/1 lb 2 oz spinach leaves, stalks removed, well washed and drained, and coarsely chopped

1 teaspoon red chilli powder

1 tablespoon cornflour

salt

ghee, to serve

1 Heat the ghee in a wok or large frying pan and sauté the green chillies and ginger for a moment or two. Add the mustard greens, spinach leaves and the chilli powder.

2 Fry, stirring all the while, until the vegetables are cooked and they release their liquids. At this stage add the cornflour, mixing it in thoroughly. Season to taste with salt. Whack the whole lot into a food processor and make a fairly coarse purée.

3 Serve with a knob of ghee melting over the greens.

Note

It is not obligatory to purée the vegetables if you prefer a whole leaf texture.

Stuffed potatoes in a mint gravy Dum aloo chutney wala

Hollowed-out potatoes are filled with a mixture of cottage cheese, cashew nuts and raisins before being heated in a spicy gravy.

serves 6

1.5 kg/3 lb 5 oz potatoes, peeled
oil for deep-frying and shallow-frying
salt and pepper

for the red onion paste

500 g/1 lb 2 oz peeled red onions
100 g/4 oz unroasted cashew nuts
25 g/1 oz fresh green chillies

for the mint and coriander paste

100 g/4 oz fresh mint leaves
100 g/4 oz fresh coriander leaves

for the ginger and garlic paste

50 g/2 oz peeled garlic
50 g/2 oz peeled ginger

for the stuffing

250 g/9 oz grated paneer (see page 183)
80 g/3¼ oz fried cashew nuts
80 g/3¼ oz raisins
a big pinch of white pepper
a big pinch of salt
a big pinch of ground cumin

1 Cut the potatoes into cylinders about 5 cm/2 inches high by 4 cm/1½ inches wide. With an apple corer, remove the centre of the potato so you effectively have a potato tube that looks like a very large piece of macaroni. Rinse thoroughly under fresh water, strain and pat dry. Heat the oil for deep-frying, add the potatoes and fry until cooked. Strain the cylinders. Cool and put to one side in the fridge.

2 To make the red onion paste, boil the onions and cashew nuts until the onions are cooked. Strain, add the chillies and grind to make a paste or purée.

3 To make the mint and coriander paste, blend the leaves together until smooth. Blend the ginger and garlic together for the third paste. Mix together all of the stuffing ingredients.

4 Heat some oil and cook the ginger and garlic paste until golden, then add the other two pastes and season with salt and pepper. If the gravy is too thick, add a little water.

5 Stuff the potatoes with the cheese mixture, then pop them in the gravy and reheat until they are hot right through.

Opposite *Panjim market, Goa.*

Right *Passing the time in Udaipur.*

Potato and tomato bhaji

This is another popular street snack, eaten at all times of the day. On the street stalls they cook this on a large round *plancha*, and you can hear the click, click, click as they chop and scrape the sizzling ingredients into a smooth red purée rather like the tomato topping of a pizza, but for practical purposes you can use a wok or a frying pan. It is usually served with thin slices of raw red onion, a wedge of lemon and a little rectangular Indian cottage loaf. There are many versions of the recipe; the principle, however, is the same. Here is my version.

serves 6

700 g/1 lb 9 oz potatoes, peeled and cut
    into cubes
vegetable oil
1 tablespoon mustard seeds
6 fresh curry leaves
4 fresh red chillies, finely chopped
1 large red onion, finely diced
ghee
500 g/1 lb 2 oz very ripe tomatoes, finely
    chopped
a pinch of ground turmeric
salt
a handful of chopped fresh coriander
    leaves
1 teaspoon garam masala (see page 61)

to serve

finely sliced red onion rings
lemon juice
ghee

1 Cook the potatoes in boiling water until tender, then drain and mash until smooth.

2 Heat a little oil in the pan and cook the mustard seeds until they crackle. Stir in the curry leaves, chillies and onion. Add some ghee and cook until the onion is soft.

3 Stir in the tomatoes, mashed potato and turmeric. Season to taste with salt and cook gently, stirring all the time with a spoon or fork, until the mixture is reduced to a thick purée. Stir in the chopped coriander and sprinkle on the garam masala.

4 Garnish with red onion rings and lemon juice. At the last minute, put a knob of ghee on each portion. Serve with bread.

Opposite *Potato and tomato bhaji and Deep-fried banana and potato balls (page 164).*

Above *Fast food, Indian style.*

Deep-fried banana and potato balls

This is typical of the kind of snacks sold in the streets throughout India.

makes about 30

400 g/14 oz potatoes, peeled and cut into
    chunks

200 g/7 oz unripe green bananas,
    steamed in their skins until soft

2 green chillies, deseeded and finely
    chopped

2 tablespoons chopped fresh coriander
    leaves

2.5 cm/1 inch piece of ginger, peeled
    and very finely chopped

1 teaspoon chaat masala (see page 61)

1 teaspoon ground coriander

a good pinch of salt

1 heaped tablespoon cornflour

100 g/4 oz very thin rice noodles or
    vermicelli, broken into tiny pieces

oil for deep-frying

1 Cook the potatoes in boiling water until tender. Drain, then transfer to a food processor or blender and process to a purée.

2 Peel the bananas and purée the flesh. Mix it thoroughly with the potato purée.

3 Mix in all the other ingredients except the rice noodles or vermicelli and the oil. Form the mixture into bite-sized balls and roll them gently in the noodle or vermicelli pieces until they are coated and look like little hedgehogs.

4 Heat the oil for deep-frying, add the banana and potato balls in batches and fry until golden brown and crispy on the outside. Drain and serve with Kachumber (see page 176).

Above left to right *On the beach at Gorai, Bombay; the green pea curry; Tess, my wife, helps me out.*

Green pea curry Hari matar masala

A great way to use fresh garden peas, which are always a little hard. You can, of course, use frozen peas. It is a very simple dish, quick to cook and great to eat.

serves 3–4

vegetable oil or ghee

2 red onions, very finely chopped

3 or 4 ripe tomatoes, finely chopped

250 g/9 oz shelled, fresh green peas

salt

1 teaspoon garam masala (see page 61)

for the masala

4 or 5 fresh green chillies

2.5 cm/1 inch piece of root ginger, peeled

3 or 4 cloves of garlic, peeled

3 or 4 dried red chillies

vegetable oil

1 Grind together the masala ingredients with enough oil to make a smooth paste.

2 Heat some oil or ghee and sauté the onions until they are completely soft. Stir in the tomatoes and continue cooking until you have a rich tomato and onion sauce.

3 Stir in the masala and cook for a further 2 or 3 minutes. Add the peas, season with salt and cook until the peas are tender.

4 Sprinkle the garam masala over the peas and serve.

Deep-fried vegetables Pakora

You can use any vegetables of your choice for this dish. They are deep-fried in a chilli-flavoured chickpea batter.

a selection of vegetables, such as
    potatoes, aubergines, onions,
    courgettes, peppers and mushrooms
vegetable oil for frying

for the batter (enough for 450 g/ 1 lb vegetables)

2 cups gram flour (chickpea flour)
1 teaspoon chilli powder
1 teaspoon salt
½ teaspoon bicarbonate of soda

1 Where appropriate, peel and wash the vegetables and then cut them into thin slices and, if you feel like it, attractive shapes.

2 Mix together the batter ingredients, adding enough water to make a thick batter.

3 Heat some oil. You can test it is the right temperature by throwing in a cube of bread; if it rises to the top bubbling, the temperature is correct.

4 Simply dip the vegetables into the thick batter, pop them into the oil and cook until they are golden and crispy.

Above *Attracting a crowd in Udaipur market, Rajasthan.*

Spicy vegetable stir-fry Subz khada masala

This is a simple stir-fry of fresh vegetables cooked with whole spices and coated in a spicy tomato gravy.

serves 4–6

150 g/5 oz red onions
100 g/4 oz carrots
100 g/4 oz red or green pepper
100 g/4 oz cauliflower florets
100 g/4 oz tomatoes
100 g/4 oz green beans
100 g/4 oz green peas
150 g/5 oz ghee
20 g/¾ oz whole red chillies, coarsely
    chopped
20 g/¾ oz coriander seeds, crushed
15 g/½ oz cumin seeds
2 teaspoons red chilli powder
1 teaspoon ground turmeric
1 teaspoon garam masala (see page 61)
200 g/7 oz tomato purée
salt and pepper
chopped fresh coriander leaves, to garnish

1 Cut the red onions, carrots, red or green pepper, cauliflower florets and tomatoes to the same size, about 12 mm/½ inch cubes or pieces; the beans should be about 6 mm/¼ inch long.

2 Heat the ghee, add the chillies and the coriander and cumin seeds and fry until the seeds crackle.

3 Stir-fry the vegetables, adding them to the pan in the following order: onions, carrots, red or green pepper, cauliflower, tomato, beans and then peas.

4 Stir in the red chilli powder, ground turmeric and garam masala, then add the tomato purée. Season with salt and pepper and continue cooking until the vegetable pieces are well coated with the gravy and either *al dente* or totally tender.

5 Serve sprinkled with chopped coriander leaves.

Spicy sweetcorn Makai tamatar nu shak

In some parts of India corn forms a part of the staple diet. It is often dried for use in the winter because it is nutritious and filling. You don't have to go through the business of soaking dried corn – this dish works perfectly well with frozen kernels. Fresh or frozen sweetcorn will be lighter and more crunchy; the dried corn version will resemble lentils or pease pudding.

serves 4

vegetable oil
½ teaspoon mustard seeds
3 or 4 chillies, split lengthways
500 g/1 lb 2 oz tomatoes, finely chopped
salt
½ teaspoon ground cumin
½ teaspoon ground coriander
½ teaspoon ground turmeric
½ teaspoon chilli powder
400 g/14 oz sweetcorn kernels
a handful of chopped fresh coriander
    leaves, to garnish

1 Heat the oil in a pan, add the mustard seeds and fry until they crackle.

2 Add the chillies and sauté for a couple of moments, then add the chopped tomatoes. Season with salt and cook over a low heat until you have almost a coarse tomato purée.

3 Stir in the powdered spices, cook for 2 or 3 minutes, then add the sweetcorn (if it looks a little dry, add a splash of water). Cook until the sweetcorn is tender.

4 Sprinkle on the chopped coriander leaves and serve.

Opposite *Spicy food for a hot climate, at Naila Dhani, Jaipur.*

Masala omelette Masala anda

Use a small non-stick omelette pan for this spicy omelette.

per person

2 large fresh eggs
salt and pepper
vegetable oil
1 teaspoon chopped green chilli
1 teaspoon finely chopped tomato
1 teaspoon finely chopped onion
1 teaspoon chopped fresh coriander
    leaves

1 Thoroughly whisk the eggs and season with salt and pepper.

2 Heat a little oil in the omelette pan and quickly stir-fry the chilli, tomato, onion and coriander. Then pour the beaten egg evenly over the pan and cook until the omelette is set. Using a spatula, fold the omelette to make a half-moon shape and serve at once.

Chutneys, Pickles and Relishes

Chutneys, Pickles and Relishes

These are an indispensable element at the Indian table, and there are literally hundreds of different recipes, from a simple coarse purée of apple, mint and coriander to mind-blowingly hot chilli pickles that have been left to cook in glass jars under the baking sun. Although, certainly in the UK, you can buy some jolly good Indian condiments, here I have included just a few simple ones which will give you an authentic taste of Indian food.

Kothmir chutney

This simple sweet and sour chutney will add some zip to any dish. It will keep in the fridge for a day or so.

1 large bunch of fresh coriander leaves
   (no stalks)
5 or 6 fresh green chillies
2.5 cm/1 inch piece of root ginger,
   peeled and chopped
5 or 6 tablespoons grated fresh coconut
½ teaspoon cumin seeds
3 or 4 cloves of garlic, peeled
a dash of tamarind purée (see page 57)
1 teaspoon coriander seeds
sugar
salt

Very simply, whack everything except the sugar and salt into a food processer and blend to a smooth paste. Add sugar and salt to taste.

Note
If you have no tamarind purée, a dash of vinegar will just about do instead.

Mint and coriander chutney

Simple to make, this is just cubes of peeled apple and handfuls of fresh mint and coriander leaves, puréed. And please don't ask me how many apples, how much mint and coriander – just mix it until it pleases you.

Raita

Raita can take many forms. It is basically natural yoghurt mixed with any of the following: chopped mint, diced tomato, grated cucumber, chopped chillies, diced fruit such as pineapple, chopped spring onions – indeed anything that you fancy, cubed, cooked beetroot *también*.

Coconut chutney

This is a superb, refreshing yet tangy chutney to accompany spiced dishes.

3 or 4 tablespoons white lentils
2 cups grated fresh coconut (if you are
    forced to use dried, soak it first for an
    hour in a little canned coconut milk)
6 or 7 whole green chillies
small bunch of fresh coriander leaves
2.5 cm/1 inch piece of root ginger,
    peeled and finely chopped
coconut milk or water
1 tablespoon coconut oil
1 teaspoon small black mustard seeds
2 fresh red chillies, finely chopped (hotter
    with seeds left in, cooler with seeds
    removed, up to you)
10–12 fresh curry leaves

1 Gently toast the white lentils in a dry frying pan without burning them.

2 Blend the fresh coconut, lentils, green chillies, coriander leaves and root ginger in a food processor with enough coconut milk or water to make a fine paste. Tip into a serving dish and then mix in the remaining ingredients.

Instant cucumber pickle

This spicy pickle can be eaten the day after it is made.

200–300 g/7–11 oz cucumber
½ wineglass of white wine vinegar
a dash of water to temper to your taste
    the strength of the vinegar
salt to taste
2.5 cm/1 inch piece of root ginger,
    peeled and cut into very, very fine dice
4 or 5 small fresh green chillies, coarsely
    chopped

1 Partly peel the cucumber lengthways, then cut it in half lengthways, remove the seeds and cut into 2.5 cm/ 1 inch batons.

2 Bring the vinegar, water and salt to the boil, add the ginger while still boiling, then add the cucumber and cook for a minute or two until the cucumber is *al dente*.

3 Cool as quickly as possible, then pop it into a clean jar with the green chillies and refrigerate. It will be ready for tomorrow night's dinner.

Tomato and chilli relish

This fresh relish is absolutely excellent eaten with fried poppadoms.

4 tomatoes
2 small red onions
4 fresh green chillies
small bunch of fresh coriander leaves (no
    stalks)
juice of 2 limes or 1 lemon
salt

Finely chop the tomatoes, onions, chillies and coriander leaves. Mix them together and season with the lime or lemon juice and salt to taste.

Pineapple chaat

Pineapple chaat has a curious, but very pleasant, sweet and sour flavour. It can be eaten as a refreshing side dish during the course of a spicy Indian meal.

a few tablespoons tamarind purée (see page 57)
1 pineapple, peeled and cut into small cubes
a small handful of chopped fresh coriander leaves (no stalks)
salt

Pour just enough tamarind purée over the pineapple cubes to lightly coat them. Mix in the coriander leaves and season to taste with salt. Serve chilled.

Kachumber

This is a fresh relish so eat it on the day that you make it.

1 red onion, finely diced
2 large tomatoes, blanched, skinned, deseeded and finely diced
about 10 cm/4 inch piece of cucumber, partly peeled, seeds removed and finely diced
a small handful of chopped fresh coriander leaves
1 or 2 green chillies, deseeded and finely chopped
a pinch of red chilli powder
salt to taste
juice or 2 or 3 lemons or limes

Mix everything together except the lemon or lime juice. Just before serving, stir in the lemon or lime juice.

Opposite from top to bottom *Sweet and sour pineapple; Onion, tomato and cucumber relish; Mango and chilli chutney (page 178).*

Mango and chilli chutney

This fruity chutney can be kept in the fridge for several days and, indeed, will improve with keeping.

6 small red shallots, finely chopped

vegetable or coconut oil

10 dried or fresh red chillies, chopped

2 semi-ripe mangoes, peeled and
    coarsely chopped

5 cm/2 inch piece of root ginger, peeled
    and very finely chopped

sugar

salt

1 Sauté the shallots in some oil until they are soft and translucent and slightly golden.

2 Stir in the chillies and continue cooking until they are soft and well mixed with the shallots.

3 Stir in the chopped mango and ginger and season to taste with sugar and salt, then simmer until you have a typical chutney consistency. Allow the chutney to cool and then refrigerate.

Sweet mango pickle

500 g/1 lb 2 oz unripe mangoes, peeled
    and cut into small finger-sized pieces
500 g/1 lb 2 oz pure cane sugar crystals
1 tablespoon red chilli powder
about ½ teaspoon salt
¾ tablespoon fennel seeds
1 shallow teaspoon fenugreek seeds
2 pinches of asafoetida

for preserving
a small amount of coconut oil
½ teaspoon small black mustard seeds

1 Mix together all the ingredients except the coconut oil and mustard seeds. Pack tightly into a screw-top jar and shut securely.

2 Place the jar in a heatproof bowl filled with water and cook gently in the oven for about 1 hour or until the whole thing has taken on a pickle consistency. Alternatively, stand the jar on a trivet in a heavy-based saucepan of water on top of the stove and simmer gently.

3 Allow to cool, then cover the top of the chutney with the oil and sprinkle the mustard seeds on the top. Re-seal and keep in a cool place for 2–3 weeks before using.

Sweets
and
Drinks

Sweets and Drinks

No festival or celebration in India is complete without sweetmeats and desserts. A lot of them are milk-based, making them also nourishing – and they're very sweet. Edible silver or gold leaf is often used to decorate the sweetmeats which adds to their festive appearance.

Yoghurt-based lassis and fresh fruit juices are popular everywhere, and Indian beer is pretty good, too!

Indian cottage cheese Paneer

If you are going to the trouble of making this cheese, it might be a good idea also to make my favourite Indian pudding, Gulab jaman, because one of the important ingredients for this dessert is a quarter of a cup of the curds (chhena) before they are pressed into cheese. So, I might as well give you the recipe for this pudding here and now – see page 184.

3 litres/5¼ pints full cream milk
about 90 ml/3⅓ fl oz lemon juice or
     vinegar

1 Put the milk in a saucepan and heat it. Just before it boils, add the lemon juice or vinegar which will curdle the milk as it comes to the boil.

2 Once the milk has curdled, turn off the heat, place a muslin cloth over a suitable-sized vessel and strain the curds and whey through the muslin.

3 Once the curds are totally drained, squeeze them into a ball in the muslin and place them under a heavy weight for 2 or 3 hours to turn it into a block that can then be cut into cubes.

Indian coconut fudge Narial barti

I suggest you buy dry coconut, add a little milk and process it in the blender to achieve the puréed coconut for this recipe.

makes about 30 pieces
60 g/2¼ oz sugar
80 ml/generous 3 fl oz water
600 g/1 lb 6 oz puréed coconut
1 teaspoon ground cinnamon
a good pinch of saffron threads
a dash of rosewater
1 heaped tablespoon finely chopped
     pistachio nuts
a couple of sheets of Indian silver leaf, to
     decorate

1 Boil the sugar and water until you have a thick syrup.

2 Add all the other ingredients except the silver leaf and mix well.

3 Pour the mixture on to a greased baking tray and lay the silver leaf over the top. Allow to set.

4 Once it is firm, cut the fudge into bite-sized pieces.

Gulab jaman

This is a pretty painstaking pudding but well worth the effort. I suggest you do the boring bit – reducing the milk – the day before.

1 litre/1¾ pints full cream milk

¼ cup of fresh curds (see Paneer, page 183)

3 tablespoons flour

a pinch of bicarbonate of soda

4 cups sugar

5 or 6 crushed green cardamom pods

2 teaspoons saffron threads

2 drops rosewater

ghee for deep-frying

1 Bring the milk to the boil, lower the heat and simmer until the milk has reduced by half. Now, stirring all the time and scraping the thickened milk from the side of the pan, let it reduce and reduce for about an hour until you have a paste-like consistency. At this stage you can refrigerate it until required.

2 Mix the curds and the thickened milk together. Stir in the flour and bicarbonate of soda and then knead it all together until you have a soft dough. Roll pieces of the dough into small balls then flatten them into discs or ovals.

3 Boil the sugar in 2 cups of water until you have a golden brown syrup and put to one side.

4 Crush the seeds from the cardamom pods with the saffron and make a coarse paste with the rosewater. Put a pinch of this filling into the centre of each disc and roll them back into balls.

5 Heat sufficient ghee in a pan and deep-fry the balls. Pop the balls into the syrup and leave to marinate in the fridge for 1–2 hours, or all day if you like. To serve, simply reheat them in their syrup in the microwave or in a saucepan.

Left Workers at the K C Das sweet factory in Calcutta.

Opposite Gulab jaman, and Indian coconut fudge (page 183).

Kulfi

This is a wonderfully sweet, rich, creamy sort of ice cream.

serves 4

1 litre/1¾ pints full cream milk
180 g/6 oz white sugar
a good pinch of saffron threads
2 teaspoons blanched pistachio nuts,
    chopped
2 or 3 green cardamom pods, coarsely
    crushed

1 Boil the milk and sugar in a heavy-based pan until reduced by two thirds and thick and creamy.

2 Turn off the heat. Add the saffron, pistachio nuts and cardamom pods and leave to cool.

3 Once the mixture is cool, pour it into 4 suitable moulds, cover with cling wrap and freeze overnight.

SARAVANAAS
Veg. FAST FOODS, FRESH JUICES,
SARAVANAA ICE CREAM.

ADAI AVIAL
VEG. CUTLET
BREAD CUTLET
ASSORTED BAJJI   12. NOON

Above *Elephant polo at the Taj Jai Hotel, Jaipur, Rajasthan.*

Fire and ice

This splendidly refreshing drink was made for me by Pritam, the excellent bartender of the Trident Hotel in Udaipur.

serves 1

1 teaspoon very, very finely chopped deseeded green chilli

1 teaspoon very, very finely chopped fresh mint

1 tablespoon fresh lime juice

2 teaspoons sugar syrup (see page 189)

1 tablespoon or so crushed ice

200 ml/7 fl oz fresh pineapple juice

for the garnish

1 fresh mint leaf

1 lime slice

In a suitable glass, put the green chilli, mint, lime juice, sugar syrup and ice. Top up with the pineapple juice and stir well. Serve garnished with a mint leaf and a lime slice. Delicious.

Note

You could, of course, reduce the quantity of fresh pineapple juice and substitute the difference with vodka. Or to hell with it. Why substitute the pineapple juice? Just slosh in the vodka.

Lassis Yoghurt drinks

Lassis are refreshing, sweet or savoury, creamy drinks made from natural yoghurt.

Sweet lassi

serves 4
1 litre/1¾ pints natural yoghurt
100 ml/4 fl oz sugar syrup (see below)
6 ice cubes
some pomegranate seeds

To make sweet lassi, mix the yoghurt, sugar syrup and ice cubes in a blender until you have a frothy, creamy mixture. Tip it into glasses and top with the pomegranate seeds.

Lassi masala

Crush together equal quantities of coriander seeds, peppercorns and cardamom seeds, enough to give you a heaped tablespoonful when they are crushed. Blend the yoghurt, as for Sweet lassi (above), with 2 teaspoons salt and a quarter of the crushed spices. Tip into glasses and garnish each glass with the remainder of the crushed spices and some chopped fresh coriander leaves.

Salt lassi

Make as for sweet lassi, but instead of sugar syrup, add 2 teaspoons of salt and omit the pomegranate seeds.

Fruit lassi

Purée any soft fruit of your choice, such as raspberries, strawberries, mangoes, apricots or bananas, to make about 250 ml/9 fl oz of purée. Add the purée to 750 ml/27 fl oz yoghurt and 100 ml/4 fl oz sugar syrup and blend as before with some ice cubes.

Note

To make sugar syrup, put 50 g/2 oz sugar (granulated or caster) in a saucepan with 300 ml/10 fl oz water. Place over a moderate heat and stir until the sugar has dissolved. Bring to the boil and simmer for 3 or 4 minutes, then remove from the heat. Leave to cool. The syrup can be stored in the fridge for several weeks.

Index